THE FINE RED LINE

THE FINE RED LINE

Stories from the Watch Room

A book by

TOM OLSHANSKI

ISBN 979-8-89109-054-5 (Paperback)
ISBN 979-8-89109-055-2(Ebook)

"Firefighters are the ones who show us that sometimes the smallest act of kindness can make the biggest difference."

—Anonymous

"A firefighter's greatest strength is their compassion for others."

– Anonymous

CONTENTS

CHAPTER 1

WELCOME TO THE WATCHROOM

What an honor to have spent a 50-year career in the fire service. During this time, I've been so honored to have shared countless stories told about firefighting by firefighters and for firefighters. Looking back, I'm so fortunate to have been able to talk to the very volunteer firefighters who responded to Flight 93 in Shanksville Pennsylvania, to meet and participate directly with the volunteer firefighters who responded to the fertilizer explosion in West Texas, to share time with the career firefighters who responded to the Oklahoma City bombing, and to meet and share time and a meal with the career firefighters who responded to the Station Nightclub fire in 2003. The stories of the fire service are endless.

My first 25 years were spent in both volunteer and career departments as a firefighter, paramedic, and officer. For the second 25 years of my career, I served as the Director of External Affairs for the United States Fire Administration. During my time with the USFA on the national front in support of all firefighters, I've shared much with my firefighter family.

Many of the stories told by media today involve large departments such as New York, Philadelphia, Baltimore, and Los Angeles, for example. But the real story to be told is one where no matter where you are, no matter where you travel you have men and women firefighters ready to respond to whatever emergency a community experiences.

When called, these men and women respond, no matter the emergency, no matter the size of the emergency, no matter the complexity of the emergency. Call and they respond, and some will, unfortunately, lose their lives in service to their communities and residents.

In these times, everyone's schedule is so busy. You get a bit of media information here or there without ever being invited behind the curtains to witness the dedication shown by the estimated 1.3 million firefighters on duty today. I was given this very opportunity throughout my career.

It's cold here at Station 5 in December. On this day in 1975, local television weather spokespersons had called for high temperatures in the low 20s. The city could also expect anywhere from a half-inch of snow up to 8 inches of snow in total. This snowstorm's impact would depend on where the snow line would go north or south of the city.

Forecasts like this one are particularly challenging for firefighters across the city and state. Small amounts of snow usually bring numerous emergencies, with car accidents and falls by residents trying to walk on slippery surfaces. This coating of a smaller amount of snow meant slick conditions, and drivers tend to speed more than during heavy snowfalls.

Heavier amounts of snow call for chains covering the wheels of the fire trucks and a lot of snow removal from around the fire stations. If snowfall predictions prevailed, sidewalks, driveways, and fire truck ramps would require constant clearing on this particular day.

No snow was falling early in the day, just cold temps and a workday beginning at 7 a.m. After getting our fire gear, helmets, and boots placed on our Medic Unit 5 and air tanks (SCBAs) checked, it was time for my partner John and I to head for coffee with the entire crew. Morning coffee was a chance to hear from the station leadership about our drill and training plans for the day. It was also time to solve the world's problems, including everything wrong in and around the city.

In the station Watch Room, we noticed someone had brought in or donated a small Christmas tree. It was placed in the Watch Room for firefighters and visitors to see and enjoy. "Well, it was supposed to be a Christmas tree anyways," they said. It was more like the model tree used for the Charlie Brown Christmas Special, and with only one ornament, it did qualify as a Christmas tree, and it was green.

In most firehouses, the two busiest areas are usually the fire station Watch Room and the station Kitchen. Firefighters typically eat two meals each day together, lunch and dinner. Our traditional breakfast was always coffee and peanut butter toast. A welcomed exception was when there were the new births of children, birthdays, and anniversaries; for example, firefighters might be rewarded with donuts by the honored person having a significant life event.

The station's Watch Room was the heart of the station. Firefighters welcomed visitors and members of the public there. The administration also hung departmental policy notices there and firefighters sold bicycle licenses; and voters sometimes registered there. Logs of daily activities are kept in the Watch Room, along with the radios and scanners to keep track of the rest of the city emergencies and fire apparatus movement. With the city fire department responding to an average of fifty to sixty calls for service during a typical day, all firefighters, especially the paramedics, needed to be aware of apparatus movements, especially those in neighboring territories.

Suppose a fire station is dispatched and gets involved in a lengthy call or a prolonged hospital patient conveyance. In that case, the surrounding stations are responsible for picking up the slack should another call come in for that original station. It's called Situational Awareness and can benefit the response of fire vehicles significantly when snow is predicted, and response to emergencies is so adversely affected by the weather.

The Watch Room is typically near the station's front door and is open to the public. Whereas the Kitchen is private and only for firefighters or invited guests. On this cold December day, the drink of choice was coffee. Although current health and safety recommendations for firefighters are to drink water and juices to stay hydrated, we only thought about intelligent things like health and safety when we were young.

We were also unaware of the dangers presented by the chemical toxins present in all smoke. These are called the products of combustion. We should have been more aware. Many veteran volunteer and career firefighters are paying the price in their senior years with poor health consequences for not paying more attention to the fluids and food they put in their bodies and the products of combustion they breathed in.

The Firehouse Kitchen is an interesting place to be. You can often hear the older firefighters talk about their experiences in response to large past emergencies. Both the young and older firefighters jointly participate in a never-ending list of discussion topics. There's a lot of storytelling, jokes, news of personal family events, the most current updated fishing reports, automobile work, sports, and relationships. The topics list is an unconstrained discussion of any and all topics. So firefighters grab a cup of java and pull up a chair to enjoy the banter and discussions by other firefighters at the kitchen table throughout the day.

The Kitchen is also a place to hear from the firefighter who is cooking for the crew and their menu plans for the day. There's also a chance to complain about the cost of a meal or a particular item on the menu. There's always a chance to tell the cook how to do something better and more efficiently or how their mother added something to a recipe. Helpers always take the opportunity to contribute to the cook's best efforts. The person who has dishwashing responsibilities after the meal also has the chance to remind the cook to use fewer pots and pans.

At the kitchen table, one quickly understands there's no problem in this world the firefighters cannot fix if given 15 minutes and a cup of coffee. Is there global strife in a far-away land? Not a problem. Firefighters have the solution and know what our politicians should or shouldn't be doing. Economic challenges, no problem. Give us another cup of coffee, and we'll have a solution. Are you going through a divorce? Not a problem. Your legal team will be gathered and at your service around the firehouse table with free advice. You have a child not doing well in school, not a problem? We can fix that as well. No problem is too big or too small for the firefighters at the station's kitchen table.

So far, on this day, we've had an easy start to our 24-hour shift. My partner John and I responded to a call for minor injuries to a young man from a slip on some ice. No conveyance was necessary. For one patient with chest pain, we administered some nitro, monitored the patient, and conveyed them to a local hospital for further evaluation.

The Engine Company crew from our firehouse also had two other calls in the morning before lunch. The first was a small fire in a vehicle motor compartment. The vehicle owner attempted to "jump start" his car battery and reversed the cables by putting negative on positive and positive on the negative. The result was the engine wires catching fire. Fortunately, the firefighters used only a fire extinguisher at this fire. Simply using water in these temperatures makes a frozen mess.

The second call for our Engine Five was gross. No other word for it, just gross. A fire erupted in the back of a full garbage truck on its way to the city's landfill/recycle center. The only way to extinguish these fires is to dump the garbage truck's load in the street, grab a hose and some pike poles and start pulling the garbage apart while spraying water on wherever there's fire. The situation was made a hundred times worse again by the cold temperatures. Ice is everywhere. Garbage is everywhere. The smell is everywhere. "Ick." Warm showers for the crew of Engine 5 were a definite must before anyone sat together for lunch.

As predicted, the snow began to fall in the mid-afternoon. With the arrival of the anticipated snow, Medic Units across the city started to get busier. Most calls for ambulances were slips and falls and an ever-growing number of fender benders across the city. Our responses also included a young man with a broken wrist at a local middle high school. It happened during a Phys Ed class game of Dodge Ball. (This call reminded everyone of the Ben Stiller movie by the same name.)

Engine Company 5 would have a couple more easy calls that afternoon. First, they were called to check the source of an interior building fire alarm. The Ladder Truck stayed inactive the entire day. The firefighters on duty were teasing the Ladder Company crew, that they would probably have to cut the cobwebs off the wheels before the ladder truck went anywhere. Finally, dinner was ready right on time, at 5 p.m. Eating a meal on time, hot, and not interrupted by emergency calls is so nice.

Several firefighters shoveled snow as the station fell into the nighttime hours. The snowfall was perfect, steady with big flakes, if there's such a thing. One could imagine that if Norman Rockwell had been there, he would have found great beauty and inspiration in this slowly arriving storm. Shoveling snow off so much station concrete is easy when done every couple of hours or several times a day. Instead of one large amount of snow to shovel, repeating the shoveling every few hours helps to keep the workload light.

Several other firefighters were in the Watch Room debating whether the new Christmas tree could hold a strand of Christmas lights. The consensus of the firefighters was no, as there was only one ornament already on the tree, and it could barely stand up. However, there was prevailing consensus on one thought that evening among the station crew was the hope our Captain wouldn't decide to put the chains on the Engine 5 and Ladder 5 wheels. It's a difficult task to get them on the Engine 5, but a monstrous effort to get them placed on the Ladder Company.

For a Friday night, it was unsettlingly quiet. With college students and public schools now closed for their holiday breaks, residents were spending more and more time in their homes. It was tranquil in the station except for the inevitable Captain's announcement over the station intercom that we would be "chaining up" the wheels for a snowfall that had no end in sight. It was better that the announcement came at 8:45 p.m. rather than 2 a.m. The station crew took about 45 minutes to get the chains on the Engine and Ladder trucks. Medic units didn't get chained up but instead would depend on studded tires for traction in the snow. One moment, please…

"Attention Engine 10, Rescue 10, Engine 8, Engine 3, and Truck 8 for a structure fire at 1431 Hayward Street with occupants trapped."

Not to worry, this call is for other stations, not ours. Once an active air force base at our airport, it fell victim to a 1971 military facilities realignment within the state during the close of Viet Nam war. The city leadership took advantage of the vacated military housing units to provide low-cost, well-maintained housing for an estimated 50 families in need.

The Hayward Street call was a typical first-alarm assignment for the department. Three Engines (Pumpers with hose and water), each with three firefighters, a Truck Company (known also as Hook and Ladder Trucks) with two firefighters, a Medic Unit (with two firefighter/paramedics), and a Battalion Chief (BC) with their driver would bring a total of seventeen fire department personnel to this call. The National Fire Protection Administration recommends in its guidelines that a minimum of seventeen firefighters respond initially to all fires on the first alarm. They would further recommend achieving this magic number by sending four firefighters on each Engine, four firefighters, including the paramedics on the Medic Unit on the Truck Company, and a Battalion Command Vehicle.

Like so many municipal fire departments throughout the country, one of the dangerous trends has been to cut back on firefighting resources during the budget process of the community. To policymakers throughout the nation, the number of firefighters is often a bottom-line budget decision. Unfortunately, these reductions continue to adversely impact the efficiency of firefighters and firefighting. Volunteer and career firefighters will be among the first to remind folks that fire trucks don't put out fires, firefighters do.

While seventeen firefighters are the guideline recommendation of the National Fire Protection Association (NFPA), the best we could do was fifteen to sixteen initially before drawing in additional support from stations much farther away and leaving large areas of the city with underserved fire protection due to the additional resource requests.

It's cold here in December. I couldn't help but feel for the firefighters just dispatched to Hayward Street....

CHAPTER 2

DANNY, DOUG, and ELIZABETH

"Attention Station 5 complete including Medic 5, Engine 1, Medic 1, and Battalion Chief, respond to 1421 Hayward Street on second alarm assignments. Use radio channel 3."

Excuse me, but now my partner John and I are part of this second alarm on Medic 5. Got to run…

Within minutes of the initial dispatch of fire units, the Officer of Engine 10 reported smoke and a yellow glow visible from over a half mile away. Upon Engine 10's arrival, radio traffic exploded in numerous transmissions, with calls for more firefighting companies and Medic Units.

"Flames are on the first floor, second floor and shooting from windows in the front and back of the living units." And then the most fearful radio transmission of all, "occupants trapped confirmed." This message would immediately prompt a second alarm being toned out citywide by the 911 Communications Center, adding two more Engine Companies, an additional Ladder Company, and two additional Medic Units.

"Children are jumping out of every second-floor window. So, we need every Medic Unit you can give us," shouted the Engine 10 Lieutenant.

By this time, firefighters were busy on the fire ground, establishing vital and secure water supplies from the nearby fire hydrants to the Engines and then from the Engines to the firefighting hoses. As water flowed and threatened to freeze, firefighters were able to make a quick fire attack, while other firefighters were rushing through snow drifts to retrieve and assist the children jumping from windows, screaming, and lying injured in the snow.

When Engine 10 reported seeing a yellow glow and smoke in the area, firefighters had already started toward their apparatus. Due to better mobility in the snow, our ambulance pulled out of fire station 5 well ahead of Engine 5 and Truck 5 into a very surreal snowy evening. Ahead of us was nothing but this beautifully peaceful snowstorm. At the same time, fire officers on the Hayward Street fire scene described the most chaotic scene of the fire, rescues in progress, and an unknown number of injured children.

The volume of radio chatter clearly indicated the fire units at the scene were busy and anxious for help. There came a request from dispatch to send two community transport Metro buses also to be brought to the scene. One could easily understand a request for heated buses as an ideal location for firefighter rehabilitation in this cold. We only knew, once we arrived on the scene, that the second alarm was ordered for children and occupants of the building. These fire survivors required a warm shelter. The second bus would later become a central location for parents of child victims to begin to receive family assistance.

The Engine and Truck would typically lead the way for fire company responses, with the Medic Unit following behind. Department leadership thought it was simpler to park an ambulance once these larger units found their necessary parking and working space around emergency scenes. However, on this night, given the distance needed to travel to Hayward Street and the immediate demand for medical services, we were ordered by the Station 5 Captain to take off ahead. Because of the snowy conditions, the Captain and Lieutenant would later explain their decisions. Both had positive comments about the decision to jump ahead rather than following the department's fire vehicle response orders. We followed the Captain's orders to take off on this evening's slippery roads with snowfall making visibility a bit difficult at high speed. Engine 5 and Ladder 5 would follow well behind us.

While the first Medic Unit 10 was committed to retrieving and treating kids in the snow they also began evaluating victim injury severity. Medic 10 requested through Fire Command that John and I on Medic 5 set up a Triage Unit on the unplowed street in front of the building. This order by command officers made perfect sense. We would set up a triage receiving area for the injured where the firefighters could bring the children they recovered. We would evaluate the victims for injuries and also hypothermia. At the same time, other responding Medic Units with paramedics and the County Medic Units with Basic Level EMTs would respond to our triage location to pick up children and convey them to one of the four Emergency Rooms in the city. While some injuries were significant, all these kids were cold and needed a place to go. Not a good situation, so additional Metro city buses were also requested to set up at the scene to provide a place of refuge with heat for the uninjured.

A firefighter carried the first child brought to our Medic Unit 5 from Truck 8 firefighters, and the child was unconscious with an apparent head injury. The child appeared to be around 10 or 11 years old. While it would be speculative as to what he struck his head against, whatever it was, it was hard. A small concrete landscape wall around this building under the snow could easily have been the cause of the head injury. On the other hand, it might have been one of the large garden boulders around the building, also snow-covered. Neither of these two garden features helped in any way to cushion the fall for these children. This child needed Advanced Life Support (ALS).

All the while, everywhere at the scene, the screaming was ear piercing with sounds of injured children, neighbors, and parents. People were hollering for children lying in the snow, trying to be sure everyone was found. Parents of some children were just beginning to arrive. It would become known after the fire that this had been a large slumber and birthday party involving the 11-year-old resident of the home and her 10 classmates. There was speculation at the scene about the exact number, but it appeared to be about sixteen kids, counting the additional family children living there. Being so close to the holidays, it was clear that the house was full of presents and decorations the kids had put up for the holiday and birthday.

As the crew delivered children to Medic Unit 5, other medic units began to arrive. These county units had traveled a distance to get to this fire but could only provide Basic Life Support (BLS). In our EMS history at that time, two types of medic units responded to emergencies throughout the state. Basic Life Support represented about 100 hours of training and focused on splinting, airway management, and fundamental first aid skills. Today these volunteers and career EMTs have cardiac and advanced airway and blood management skills. Unfortunately, that wasn't the case when this fire occurred.

The second type of service was Advanced Life Support or ALS. As highly trained paramedics, we have received 7 months of training in the University Medical School and several months of in-field training. Paramedics were trained to work closely with local emergency rooms and perform advanced treatments for critically ill or injured patients. Those skills included intubation, defibrillation, and administering about 35 different medications (including morphine) that one didn't see in a local pharmacy but instead on the local hospitals' "crash carts."

The county voluntary EMS units were invaluable in treating those children requiring stabilization of fractures, warming, and burn care. The other children requiring advanced life support due to significant burns or compromised airways would be transferred to arriving ALS paramedic units for treatment and conveyance to local hospitals.

The Hayward Street fire scene was incredibly confusing. No one was sure of the children's names or where patients were being transported. Their parents were asking and wanted to know where their children were. Fortunately, the hospitals were coordinating amongst themselves who could take what child, and what level of care was required to maximize the survivability of the children. The hospitals were instructed to notify the 911 Center of patient names as they got them so that information could be relayed to the fire ground and given to arriving parents trying to find their child.

Medical treatments were administered through our Medic Unit 5 triage setup, and the firefighters from Stations 10, 5, 3 and 8 could now focus on fire extinguishment coordinated with the two on-scene truck companies. Advancing a hose full of water through the snow continued to make attacking the fire very difficult for firefighters. The Battalion Chief who had just arrived was screaming into the radio orders for this and that to be done. We had no fire scene command structure at that time, but that would change soon after this fire with the department-wide integration of the Incident Command System (ICS).

Incident Command System was designed to provide an organized fire ground operation structure firefighters could effectively operate efficiently and safely. ICS is an understood system that when used in chaotic situations like this one, with planned tactical orders, would provide strategically determined and coordinated tasks for fire crews attacking fires. This particular chief who had just arrived was what my fellow firefighters referred to as "old school" or "dinosaur." Just throw a bunch of firefighters at a fire, and it'll eventually go out. Of course, we know much differently today, but back to the Hayward Street fire.

When firefighters entered the front door of the burning residence, they immediately entered a small foyer. Straight ahead were the stairs to the second floor. Taking an immediate right, they would enter the living room, dining room, and Kitchen. Engine 10 firefighters had one of two decisions to make. They could immediately go to the right and enter the living room, where the fire had started and was burning freely uncontrolled or go straight into an enclosed stairwell full of fire. The stairwell, once again, led directly to the second floor.

There was a report that all of the children had been accounted for, except for two young boys and a tiny 3-year-old girl, Elizabeth. All three were the children of the homeowners. The two older boys of the family, ages 16 and 13, were named Danny and Doug, respectively. All missing.

As firefighters from Engine 10 and 3 entered the home, they immediately faced fire, intense heat, and smoke in the living room and the staircase. A quick spray of water into the living room would knock down the fire and cool the heat slightly until other firefighters entered the back door through the Kitchen. While they may have stayed in the front foyer putting out the fire on the first floor, their primary mission was to reach the unaccounted-for children presumed to still be on the second floor.

The free burning heat and smoke from the fire in the enclosed stairway was intense. So intense it would keep firefighters from immediately trying to ascend the stairs. The fire from the second floor and stairwell formed a tunnel of fire. Even with their protective equipment and breathing apparatus and water, it appeared nearly impossible to reach the second floor by crawling on hands and knees, dragging their hose through the intense fire conditions facing them.

A small figure suddenly appeared as these firefighters sprayed water into the stairwell. Walking down the stairs was the 3-year-old girl, Elizabeth. She walked straight into the arms of the firefighters. She was dressed in only her nightclothes and was barefoot. While wet from the spray of water, Fred and Steve had shot up into the stairwell, this child had walked through the fire and smoke. No marks. No burns. Not even burned hair or feet. Just a face and arm blackened by smoke and soot. To this day, no explanation has been given or even attempted. Miracles happen, and the men and women of the fire service see them often. This one miracle had indeed been witnessed by Fred and Steve that night at the bottom of the stairwell. The Almighty had spared a child this night.

Firefighters brought Elizabeth to my partner and me at Medic 5. My partner John examined her from head to toe, and she was without a single mark or burn. Her clothing smelled of smoke, as did the rest of her. The fire crew confirmed that neither a burn nor tear of any kind was on her clothing. Making this even more astounding, the crew found out later the child had an epilepsy condition.

Eventually, firefighters would reach the second-floor bedroom, where they would find the burned bodies of the two missing boys in what appeared to have been a bunk bed. The fire had consumed the mattresses and covers, and the boys' bodies were found together wedged between two box springs. It's unknown whether the boys were responsible for helping kids get out of windows or if they simply focused on protecting one another prior to their deaths.

The bottom line, fire kills. It's a gruesome way to die. Firefighters at this scene chose to believe that they passed as heroes that night, saving other children before becoming fire death statistics. Hopefully, and this is sad to say, the smoke rendered them unconscious before the flames consumed the bed and the boys. One cannot imagine a more horrific death than by fire.

The real purpose of telling this story was to describe what firefighters Fred and Steve experienced as they attempted to move up to the second floor and then found the two boys clutching one another, burned beyond recognition. As described earlier, the stairway was enclosed and burning. Sadly, this created a perfect chimney for smoke and fire to travel to the second floor.

That night, a week before Christmas, our fire department witnessed firsthand what some might call a miracle. The firefighters on duty the night of the Hayward Street fire have no other words for what they witnessed. Some have said this was blind chance occurrence for Elizabeth, or those firefighters just made up this story. Nope. It's the story of two firefighters who were in this fire and witnessed this miracle firsthand.

Our department of over 260 personnel only had the description of what the firefighters witnessed firsthand and the miraculous perfect condition of the child, and that remains with no other explanation. There was a Higher Hand involved that night.

The cause of the fire was determined to be a candle on a small table which was moved too close to some window coverings in the dining room. One of the children had moved a candle to make more room for a sleeping bag. The decorations and drapes caught fire. The house was full of children, mainly on the second floor. It was a holiday slumber party, and most of the kids were from the immediate area housing. The living room was full of Christmas decorations and a very dry Christmas tree. When the flames met the drapes, this once quiet, snowy, peaceful night would become a part of the tragic memories for a lifetime for so many victims and parents.

There are many odors that volunteer and career firefighters tune into for their safety. Accelerants like gas, alcohol, and others. Odors that indicate hydrocarbons, such as burning tires or diesel fuel, are involved. The smells indicate lumber or paper products burning. The sense of smell is critical to all firefighters as the odors add one more piece to the puzzles of the emergencies and chaotic environments volunteer and career firefighters are being called to work in.

There are two odors that are unmistakable to firefighters and EMS personnel. The first horrific odor is that of human flesh decomposition. No further explanation is needed but to say it's terrible, and once you first experience and catch wind of the smell, it stays with you for a lifetime. The second (and takes first place for far too many firefighters) is the smell of burning or burnt human flesh. Again, these odors last for a lifetime of tragic memories.

When the firefighters reached the second floor, there was no mistaking the odors of burned victims. Danny and

Doug were quickly found in the bottom of their bunk beds. Doug was wrapped in Danny's arms, maybe to protect each other or as a final gesture of love. Perhaps the boys had taken refuge there, thinking it was safe. Maybe before hugging, they were able to help others out of the windows. Unfortunately, there's no way to know what was done or how or why they ended up in the bunk bed. The box spring from the upper bunk and bunk bed structure itself had been almost totally consumed by the fire, enough so that the remaining springs fell on to the two boys. They were both in each other's arms, burned beyond recognition, and both dead. Simply HELL.

As volunteers and career firefighters know and feel all too often, even one death by fire is a failure of the fire department to achieve its core mission to save lives. Property can be replaced but lives......never. When a firefighter or EMTs loses their life, the nation and family of all firefighters mourn the failure to achieve the national goal of "Everyone Goes Home." Firefighters and members of the public.

Former Pittsburgh Bureau of Fire Chief, and former Deputy United States Fire Administrator, Charlie Dickinson often explains and compares these tragic events to be like "links of a chain." If someone could have broken just one of the links in this tragic chain of death, these two boys would still be able to celebrate birthdays, graduate schools, possibly marry and have children, or simply achieved their life goals, not end their lives as just another fire statistic. No individual is born with a goal to be a fire death statistic.

This fire scene had many possible breakable links. What if real candles had not been used or the candle had not been moved? What if there were no flammable draperies or there were batteries in the smoke detectors? What if the buildings had installed sprinkler systems and there had been a home escape plan that everyone practiced? These possible scenarios where a link could have been broken are endless. Yet, the links aligned perfectly this night to take these fire victims across the fine line between life and death, These scenes are witnessed daily by volunteer and career firefighters. There's a very fine line between being here breathing one second and gone, dead, deceased the next second.

In 1972, a couple of years before I joined the career firefighter ranks, as many as six to seven thousand residents of our nation lost their lives annually to fire. That is equivalent to forty-five airline crashes of Boeing 737-300 airliners, most commonly in service today. Imagine the public outrage if the people in this nation were to experience forty-five airline tragedies a year and what their resulting demand for safety and protection from such accidents would be. At the same time, in 1973, an average of more than three hundred firefighters were also losing their lives in the line of duty annually. That would add to the estimated forty-five crashes above, another two filled planes with firefighters.

Let's take these statistics one step further. These men, women, and children whose lives were lost all belonged to families. Firefighters have families, also. Hopefully, one can see the human suffering and the toll on this country with these unimaginable losses. Many of the firefighters who were at this fire had young children at home.

In 1973, the National Commission on Fire Prevention and Control, under then President Nixon, issued their final report entitled *America Burning*. As a direct result of this specific report, countless fire service leaders, engineers, safety experts, investigators, educators, and volunteer and career firefighters focused their never-ending commitment and dedication to reducing civilian fire losses.

Through the expertise and efforts of so many, and even in light of population growth, the statistics have been reduced to approximately three thousand fire deaths a year. Firefighter line-of-duty deaths are statistically average of about one hundred a year. Still, this is the equivalent of twenty-five airline crashes a year, yet we as a nation continue to accept these statistics and losses. No one comes into this world to become a statistic.

When you go to sleep at night, make sure you and your loved ones are protected by smoke alarms. And ensure bedroom doors are closed shut.

"Firefighters are the ones who bring hope to a hopeless situation."

—Anonymous

CHAPTER 3

HSSSSSSSS

On this day, my partner Steve and I on Medic 1 had just completed a patient conveyance to a local downtown hospital when our portable radio announced, "Attention Medic 1 and Engine 6, respond to 1720 Jefferson St. for an individual attacked by a snake."

"Snake!!" Did the dispatcher say the word "Snake?" "A SNAKE?!"

What in the hell are we being sent to, and why couldn't the ambulance normally assigned to this address be available? I know, I know, the first run territory was uncovered by EMS because Medic Unit 6 was on another call. Steve and I were the first backup and next to be called for a SNAKE. Just using the word "snake" was horrifying to me. I know there are many folks in this world who appreciate and understand these creatures, but I'm not one, admittedly.

As was the custom of the department, units were dispatched first. Then while en route to the emergencies, the dispatchers would provide any additional information they could gather regarding the emergency from the 911 caller.

This information could come from the victims, bystanders, police, or other sources of information.

While we were responding to Jefferson Street, the dispatcher filled us in with additional information from the caller to 911. A neighbor who called from the patient's house said a snake was "eating" a female at this location. "Holy crap." What are we getting ourselves into? We inquired what kind of snake it was, as if it mattered, and our dispatcher told us that no one had identified the type of snake to the 911 Communications Center.

Our paramedic training and state certifications to be a paramedic took roughly 8 months of intense classroom, hospital-clinic time, and supervised field experience. Between Steve and I, we couldn't even remember a nanosecond of training regarding snakes. At best, we would have to depend on something from our scout training as kids or an expert the 911 could get on the phone for us. "Really, snake?... Yes, a snake. WTF are we getting into?"

Oh my God, just mentioning a snake makes my skin crawl (no pun intended). I'm very respectful to understand that many people are free from the burden of fear of snakes. I, however, don't even like using worms while fishing. Without the ability to take time off at this point for a reasonable excuse, like a vacation or sick time, we continued our journey to the Jefferson Street address. At the same time, we (actually me) tried in vain to figure out how my partner (Steve) was going to solve this victim's emergency of being eaten by a snake, while his partner (me) waited patiently in our Medic Unit. Fortunately, several area police units and Engine 6 were simultaneously dispatched to the home ahead of us. To this day, I swear my partner drove to this emergency address way too fast. "Just saying."

While en route to the scene, we tried to figure out if either of us had any experience with snakes. No experience. Fortunately with Engine 6 expected to arrive ahead of us, hopefully, they would be able to evaluate and get the scene under control by the time we got to the home. However, only a short time after Engine 6 arrived, they radioed their update to us. The Engine 6 Captain informed us that a large snake, believed to be a python, had indeed attempted to swallow its owner. A bit exaggerated, but a great description in my book. I have no idea what this looked like to Engine 6, but it was a good description for Steve and me.

As we turned onto Jefferson Street, you couldn't help but notice immediately the four police cars and Engine 6 parked in front of the residence. We left the medic unit, grabbed our medical boxes, and walked slowly up to the house. The stairs in the front of the house were lengthy, and the walk up to the house took a bit of time. Along the walkway, we encountered a police officer, and we immediately pointed out to her that it was odd to see her outside the home. Instead, she should be inside the home with her gun and shooting the snake. The officer could only say was this was a "very big snake." Well, okay, we'll walk a little slower.

The homes on Jefferson Street were built shortly after World War II to accommodate the many families and homebuyers returning from the war and moving into the area. Generally, these were single-story residential homes—your typical two and three-bedrooms, with a living room, kitchen, and back porch type residence.

Upon entering through the front door, we passed into the living room where we found a 30-year-old female lying on a couch in a fetal-type position crying hysterically. Her arm ran down along the couch to the floor, where her hand disappeared into the mouth of an 8-to-10-foot python. What the hell do we do? Most importantly, what was my partner going to do? With so many police officers present, the shooting of the snake seemed the obvious solution to me. The patient would have none of that talk, however.

The snake lived in its own bedroom in the home. An entire bedroom was remodeled and dedicated to the snake's habitat. In the room was basically a floor-to-ceiling tree-looking structure with other materials like bedding commonly used for a snake's habitat throughout the room. The snake had free roam of its bedroom and, at times, the entire house according to the owner. Allowing the snake to roam the whole house was a huge surprise when police found a newborn 3-week-old baby girl in a third bedroom.

We would learn later that Pythons have very bad vision. We were dealing with the result of a hungry snake looking for a meal. As pythons hunt by heat signatures and given that the woman's hand was on the floor while she was napping, the snake apparently mistook her hand for a rodent, its frequent meal.

As the snake approaches any meal, the Python dislocates its jaw to accommodate the size of the meal. I'm sure there's another biological term for this eating habit, but for me, any more information would be too much information. As the snake moved over the victim's hand, it could move forward with its small angular teeth. However, pythons don't have a reverse gear, so once over the hand, realizing it's not a meal, it couldn't simply let go. In conclusion, the victim's hand was trapped in the snake's mouth.

As we approached the woman on the couch with a snake's mouth over her hand, it was clear, looking at the snake, that the snake was probably more confused than we were about what was about to happen. Someone in the room voiced another request to shoot it, but it seemingly went unheard. Clearly, I wasn't loud enough. We really didn't know what to do, but fortunately, the challenge wasn't a life-threatening situation or a safety issue but simply the challenge to get the Python off the owner's hand.

Following a lengthy discussion regarding our dilemma, fortunately, on Engine 6 that day was a firefighter on duty who, indeed, was an outdoorsman and hunter. Firefighter Ron had spent much of his time in the wild when he was off-duty and came up with an idea that made sense for some reason. We would hold the snake still, which didn't appeal to me immediately, and as we did, Ron would then pry open the snake's jaws long enough for our patient to remove her hand. There, Ron solved the problem. Ron then instructed two paramedics and four police officers to hold the snake while he separated the snake's jaw from the woman's hand.

Holding onto the snake was like holding onto an 8-inch steel pipe. Ron didn't want the snake's muscles to be constricted for some reason. Whatever constriction means. The six Ron-appointed holders of the snake quickly realized how strong these creatures were. No matter how much force we used to restrict the snake's movement, in all honesty, the snake could have moved us wherever the snake desired.

We all acted so bravely, holding onto the snake in the belief that we were somehow helping Ron achieve his jaw-prying open feat. WAIT a moment… It worked. Ron successfully opened the snake's jaws, allowing the woman to pull her hand out of the snake's mouth. To finish the job, Ron immediately taped the snake's jaws closed. To this day, we don't believe the snake needed 4 yards of medical tape to secure its mouth, but who are we to judge? I was just excited not to have to try and hold the snake down anymore. We were taking no chances, and the scene was now secure and our victim free.

Unfortunately for the owners of the snake, with a 3-week-old baby in the home, this emergency response immediately raised the concern of the law enforcement officers on the scene. As a result, it was determined by law enforcement and possibly a phone call from Social Services that the snake would have to be removed from the home.

In conclusion, we were able to transport the woman into the Emergency Room for a tetanus shot and some simple wound care to her hand and wrist. The snake was taken by police officers to the Municipal Zoo and entered their new Reptile House inventory. As harsh as this may have sounded, being placed in a zoo against the owner's wishes, this could have been an entirely different emergency had their infant child been playing on the floor that day.

In the United States, there are approximately 33,000 fire departments. Ours was but one of these departments. There are also approximately 1.3 million firefighters working to deliver their fire services throughout the country. Somewhere around 72% of these fire departments are all-volunteer firefighter departments. These volunteer departments are made up of men and women community members dedicated to the safety and well-being of their fellow residents.

Nationally, there are approximately 28,000,000 calls for fire department services annually. Or about 80,000 emergency calls every day. Whether it's a snake, a bad vehicle crash, a raging fire, or even tornadoes, these men and women will respond when called upon. No fire department has ever put a sign out front of their station saying, "We won't respond to cardiac arrests today" or "We answer all calls except vehicle rollovers today." You'll never see signs like that in front of fire stations. Regardless of the reason or emergency, these men and women respond when they get the call to respond.

One of the greatest stories demonstrating the steadfast dedication of all volunteer firefighters was of the courageous actions of a small community group of volunteer firefighters who left their places of employment to respond to the airline crash of a Boeing 757, outside of their town, on the local mountain top.

The date was September 11, 2001. While the world was witnessing the events live from the New York Twin Towers, these men and women were sifting and working through the chaos and wreckage of Flight 93 in Shanksville, PA. Their actions speak directly to every firefighter's dedication and commitment to the emergencies they're called to respond to. Like so many other examples, their Flight 93 story is a true testament and a reminder to us of the incredible value of having volunteer and career firefighters on watch in your community 24 hours a day, 7 days a week.

"Firefighters are like the roots of a tree, they hold everything together when everything else falls apart."

—Anonymous

CHAPTER 4

THERE BUT FOR THE GRACE OF GOD...

Firefighters are a family. Like all families throughout the nation, firefighters can share many funny stories of practical jokes played. For 24 hours, 8-10 days a month, firefighters live, work, compete, struggle, and, sometimes, even play together. Play might involve plastic insects in meals, small holes in plastic glasses, causing unappreciated fluids to drip onto uniforms, or even rubber bands around the sink sprayers. There are just as many examples as there are volunteer and career firefighters.

When you're a firefighter, you belong to your departmental family of firefighters as well as the national firefighting family. Regardless of your travels or the emergency, you can always turn to the local jurisdictional fire department for help if you're a firefighter. It's most common for firefighters to visit other community fire stations when traveling. Whether it's for work or pleasure, firefighters who enjoy dropping into local fire stations are immediately reminded of the bigger firefighting family they're part of.

Today was a particularly cold November day. The City was quieting down as Thanksgiving was slowly approaching. There were twelve on duty in Station One. It wasn't the norm to have only twelve personnel on duty. With sick leaves and vacations elsewhere in the city stations, Station One would usually "ship out" or "detail" one or two of its firefighters to other stations to avoid overtime costs while ensuring enough firefighters on each fire department vehicle.

Jim was a ten-year veteran of the department assigned to driving Ladder 1. Ken was assigned to driving Engine 1. I don't believe there were ever better drivers and operators of these vehicles. The pride they took in their vehicles' operational readiness and appearance was admirable, as well as an assurance of safety for all the firefighters who had to work from these vehicles during emergencies.

During morning coffee before starting our station work, the four firefighters of Ladder 1 were called out to a broken water pipe in a downtown office building basement. The flooding in the basement required some of the specialized heavy-duty equipment our additional unstaffed standby Utility Vehicle carried on board. The crew of Ladder 1 left the coffee table and took the utility vehicle with them to the flooded basement.

Before Ladder 1 could return, Engine 1 was dispatched to a car fire in a parking ramp a few blocks away. Upon the Engine's return, the Station One crew, as usual, were curious to hear what they had done on their car fire run. It's a time-honored tradition in fire stations to hear about emergency runs and share together the experiences and any lessons they may learned. The firefighting family of Station One was finally back together and drinking coffee by 0930.

We were fortunate to have Jim assigned to our Station and crew for 5 years. He was a hard-charging farm boy from a rural area and a poster child for service to the community. Jim was a talented firefighter looking forward to applying for the position of fire department paramedic. Jim was married, with a wonderfully supportive wife and two small children. As if his life needed to be busier, Jim also pursued his Baccalaureate of Science in Zoology from the local university, one class at a time.

A sense of great pride exists among firefighters for their fire vehicles. If cared for and well-maintained, fire trucks can typically provide about 20 years of front-line response service, sometimes even longer. At the end of their service life, many of these well-maintained vehicles end up as reserve fire apparatus, able to be pressed back into service for short periods if and when necessary.

Apparatus Engineers (drivers) exemplify this fire vehicular pride. Can you imagine a community parade without fire trucks? A community celebration? In the fire service, care and pride for their fire apparatus exist in all departments nationwide. The members of the Station or the public, when they stop and visit a fire station, are typically there to see the trucks and equipment. They don't care where the firefighters eat or sleep. The general public enjoys climbing into and sitting in a fire truck, especially children. Parents like to see their children climb on vehicles. And enjoy the photos.

When driving on the streets and roads of the community and you see a police car, where's the first place you look? The speedometer. How fast am I going? Am I within the speed limit? When you see a fire truck, you wave like all your vehicle passengers, especially children do. The kids will likely pump their arms, hoping the fire truck driver will blow a horn or siren. Witnessing people's safe feelings around fire vehicles and firefighters has always been impressive.

Once mid-morning coffee ended, firefighters returned to their daily assignments and duties. As Jim and Ken returned to care for their fire apparatus, Ken discovered a couple of large bolts and nuts under Engine 1. "Holy crap!" This situation couldn't be. Where had these nuts and bolts come from? Goodness, his Engine 1 was falling apart. Something bad must have happened in that earlier car fire call. With a mechanic's creeper in hand, Ken went under Engine 1.

Our estimate, Ken was under his vehicle for a good 25 minutes searching for where these nuts and bolts fell from. Eventually, he asked Jim to assist with his "nuts and bolts" search. There were now two firefighters on creepers under Engine 1. Another 25 minutes passed by. Where had these bolts come from? Having yet to find where they had come from, only one alternative remained for Ken. With his chin on the floor, Ken went into the Captain's office to explain what he had found or, worse yet, not found, under Engine 1.

The Captain followed Kenny back to the vehicle to examine the bolts and nuts found under the truck. After another 15 minutes with three firefighters on mechanic creepers under Engine 1, the Captain summoned the Engine 1 firefighters to report to the apparatus floor. The firefighters were loaded up, and the Captain, Ken, and the rest of the Engine crew were off to the Bureau of Maintenance to determine where these nuts and bolts had come from. This series of events escalated very quickly. Within an hour, at least three and possibly more firefighters were under Engine 1. It had to be a record of some kind. And as expected, the Bureau of Maintenance couldn't find where the nuts and bolts might belong.

Rumors circulated throughout the crew that day that someone may possibly have used the nuts and bolts as a gag. We, as firefighters/paramedics, can neither confirm nor deny. The word was often spoken by the Captain suggesting, if true, "suspension." This threat was used far too many times for anyone to speak up. It didn't necessarily mean we did or knew anything. For heaven's sake, any number of people had been in the Station to resupply the rescue units and could have done something. Enough said about this, and time to move on. Jim smiled differently that day, and I suspect those nuts and bolts are still in an old firehouse desk somewhere.

The new station fire alarm (a doorbell taped to the 911 dispatch console) pierced the silence of the station solitude at 8:15 p.m. that evening.

"Engines 1, 3, and 4, Ladders 1 and 6, Medic Units 1 and 4, and Battalion Chief 34 to the 100 block of Drake Street for a report of fire and smoke in the building."

The address given is a YMCA facility located directly on the university campus. The building is six stories high and primarily constructed of steel and concrete blocks. The paramedics are very familiar with this building as many homeless citizens are housed there. Given the current temperatures outside, one could expect a very high occupancy count in the six-story structure. Ken, driving Engine 1, would lead the parade of Station One's firefighting units to the fire building. Typically, Ladder 1 would lead the way to the fire buildings, except, in this case, several Ladder 1 firefighters were delayed by taking evening showers. Given the potentially high occupancy considerations and the need to establish an ample water supply from fire hydrants, Engine 1 would get the go-ahead to lead Station One units.

Engine 4 and Medic 4 would arrive just moments ahead of the Station One units. The firefighters of Engine 4 reported to all the other responding units that smoke was visible from the building's exterior. An occupant evacuation was underway and being organized by the YMCA staff. In anticipation of a working fire, once Station 4 firefighters conducted the initial size-up, they turned their attention to securing a large water source. They passed their command to the Captain of Engine 1.

The department's Incident Command System (ICS) is a nationally recognized approach for most fire departments for the command, control, and coordination of emergency response resources while providing a chain of command within the chaos of any emergency. This system, and another one called Unified Incident Command System, makes it possible to be coordinated for every emergency, from a dumpster fire to a major hurricane.

As the Captain of Engine 1 remained with his fire truck to serve as Incident Commander, the other three Engine 1 firefighters grabbed a preconnected hose from Engine 4 and proceeded into the stairwell through a side door. At ground level, the environment was all clear. The firefighters of Ladder 1 then joined the Engine 1 crew. The Captain had ordered the Ladder 1 crew to begin primary and secondary room searches for potential victims on the fire floor.

When the firefighters reached the third-floor landing, the smoke conditions were miserable. The third floor was clearly the fire floor. The floor where the fire was located. Hopefully, the fire hadn't extended to any of the floors above. Visibility could only be described as total blindness. One could feel the heat generated by the fire on our necks. With the firefighter's protective clothing worn then, the neck was the only exposed skin area. With these conditions, it was important to work in pairs. Working in pairs reduces the chances of a firefighter getting separated or lost in these terrible and deadly fire conditions. Stay together.

The third-floor landing had become crowded as firefighters stopped long enough to "mask up" with their SCBA breathing masks and open the airflow from their tanks. Once turned on, the firefighters would have approximately 30 minutes of air. The Firefighters knew that the time on tank air was much shorter with heavy breathing and physical energy exertion. The final step before their entry into the third floor was to have the hose lines "charged" with water. Firefighters brought two hose lines up the stairs empty. Hose lines are much easier to manage on winding staircases when they're empty of water. Once charged with water, hose lines become heavier, stiffer, and harder to advance or move by firefighters.

Fortunately, the third-floor entry door was open, and the fire was located quickly in the second room down the long hallway on the left. The open door would make the fire attack more efficient than crawling on hands and knees down these lengthy building hallways.

Jim got to the door or the fire first and forced it open with his shoulder and a pry bar. Other firefighters waited for Jim with their hose. It was difficult, but Jim could pry and push the door open just enough to squeeze a hose nozzle into the crack of the door and give the room a quick dose of water. Jim then went about pushing on the door again. The door shouldn't have been that difficult to open. However, something was blocking the door. Another firefighter joined Jim to push open the door. It then became obvious why the door had been so difficult to open.

Jim reached around the partially open door into the fire room and discovered the reason. The room's occupant, a man in his 50s, had been lying on the floor directly behind the door—a human doorstop. With more effort, Jim was able to grab the fire victim, yank him by his shirt out of the room and drag him back to the third-floor landing. It was clear, Jim intended to get this fire victim down to the ground floor to the awaiting paramedics.

The fire victim was lifeless and very severely burned. The man had an estimated 70% second- and third-degree burns on his body. His face was blackened by soot, particularly around his mouth and nose. He had likely also inhaled actual fire possibly causing severe respiratory burns. It was clear the fire victim had also inhaled a lot of smoke.

At this point, the third-floor firefighting activities suddenly grew very confusing. Whether Jim was dragging the male down the stairs, or he attempted to carry the man, his boots got tangled up with the fire hose in the stairwell. As a result, Jim and his fire victim suddenly fell around 25 feet down a flight of stairs to the second-floor landing.

During Jim's fall, Jim lost his helmet and landed directly on his back, striking his head hard on the concrete floor. Unfortunately, he was still wearing his SCBA air tank, so landing on his back is a misstatement. In reality, Jim landed directly on his air tank. While third-floor firefighters continued to fight what became a controlled "room and contents" fire, other firefighters were now scrambling to assist Jim.

When my partner Steve and I got to Jim's side, he was unconscious. We realized quickly Jim's injuries would require a complete patient immobilization on the second-floor landing before moving him. This procedure would protect his neck and spinal cord from movement. There was no reason to know for sure, but firefighters on the first floor, coming to the aid of those fighting fire on the third floor, swore they heard Jim's head hit the second-floor concrete landing. Jim's fall was apparently that loud.

All firefighting crews, in agreement with their command officers, are trained to prioritize their tasks when involved in chaotic and dangerous environments. As it was with our department, when Medic 1 got to Jim's side, we were also dealing with the male fire victim who fell with Jim onto the same second-floor landing. Which victim do you work on first while awaiting other paramedic assistance from Medic 4 to arrive on the landing?

Our decisions were made easier when it became most apparent the fire victim was DOA (dead on arrival). Without breathing, no pulse, and such significant burns, the chances of surviving long-term weren't possible, even if successful resuscitation had been possible. Jim needed our attention immediately.

Before anything could happen, we needed to remove Jim's SCBA. Medic 4 arrived with their medical case, a backboard, and a cervical neck brace. Station 6 medics were responsible for removing the fire fatality to the outside and the cover of a yellow blanket. We made the decision to stabilize Jim's neck and spine by holding him straight and steady, removing the SCBA, and placing him on a backboard for further immobilization in three moves.

Working as a team, we first cut one strap of his SCBA harness and rolled him on his side. That allowed the opportunity to remove Jim's air tank and harness. Jim was then rolled back onto the backboard, a cervical collar applied, and then Jim was strapped tightly to the backboard. Jim may have had a hospital preference, but this night he had been on duty and was a member of our firefighter family. He was going to the Level One Trauma Emergency Room regardless of how anyone else may have felt.

While still wrestling with the fire hose in the stairwell, Jim was carefully carried down to the first floor and then to ground level. Even though Jim was unconscious throughout all of this and not a light guy, especially still in firefighting gear, spirits were raised when we ran some preliminary checks that the Trauma Center Doctor had requested by radio. While unconscious, it appeared to us that Jim showed feeling in all four extremities. As we left on a slow journey to the Trauma Center to avoid unnecessary movement in the back of the ambulance, the Battalion Chief asked us to stay at the hospital with Jim until other fire department leadership arrived at the ER, along with his family and for us to radio him from the hospital once we knew anything regarding Jim's condition.

The department leadership (Chief and Assistant Chiefs) arranged for Jim's wife to be escorted and transported to the ER. As a reminder, all family members of our firefighters, who support these men and women emotionally, are also the extended fire service family members. By driving Jim's family to the emergency room, the risk of the family having an accident trying to rush to the hospital was eliminated.

It was such a relief for Steve and me to be called into the exam room by the nursing staff to see that Jim, although surrounded by medical personnel, was awake but somewhat confused by his surroundings and able to address each of us by name. We were so relieved that he could acknowledge Steve and me before his immediate family arrived.

The Battalion Chief was updated as instructed, and most importantly, so was Jim's Station One crew. Soon, Jim's family, including his parents, as well as the fire department leadership began arriving. Jim was in the tremendous caring hands of these gifted medical professionals and would spend the rest of the night undergoing scans and tests. Finally, it was time for Medic 1 to return to Station One where these events had all started, and to help the entire firefighting crew clean up and prepare for their next potential calls. There was still a night of emergency coverage ahead of us.

It was also critical for all firefighters on duty at this time to immediately call their loved ones at home. The local media had covered this fire at the YMCA for their evening late-night news. While details were not completely known, the media had reported a death and an injured firefighter. Therefore, it was critically important for all on-duty firefighters to call loved ones and assure them they were fine and okay. The need for families to know that their firefighter is okay is of the utmost importance. Enough bad things can happen involving local fire departments, so keeping loved ones guessing is wrong and often leads to potentially long-term relationship damage.

The department's fire investigators determined the male fire fatality had been smoking in bed and either fell asleep or was too inebriated to know differently. The follow-up autopsy by the coroner would fill in those missing pieces of information. The occupant had also been a bit of a hoarder, so there was plenty of stuff to burn in the room he was occupying. The mattress caught fire and spread quickly throughout the room. Had there been a fire sprinkler system in the building, the male might still be alive, and certainly, Jim wouldn't have sustained his life-threatening injuries.

During the early morning coffee, while awaiting the new day's on-duty crew to arrive, Jim's crew was given an update. During the night, Jim suffered a small seizure while being examined and scanned. Doctors had decided to place Jim in a medically induced coma and move him into the neurological intensive care unit of the hospital. His pulse and breathing were fine, but doctors were concerned about a small amount of bleeding in his brain. As his crew members, we knew Jim was a tough son of a bitch and would come through this okay, and we were most thankful we took the time to properly care for his head and spine on the second-floor landing.

Over the next few weeks, we discovered that Jim had suffered a significant head injury and messed up some of his spinal vertebrae by landing on his air tank (SCBA). Unfortunately, it was too early to know whether these injuries were temporary or permanent. Likewise, it was too early to know the extent of the head injury or if the symptoms of the head injury would be temporary or permanent. So, all we could do the next day on duty was to think positively about our compadre and be thankful that we got him safely to the Trauma Center and into the best care possible.

Over the next several weeks and months, we received periodic updates regarding Jim, his injuries, and his recovery. During one of the briefings, it was sad and concerning for our Station One crew to hear that Jim was having extreme difficulty walking. With the help of physical therapy, he could walk with a medical walker or a cane. He was having a lot of cognitive challenges due to his significant brain injury, and it would be affecting him for the time being, and possibly for the rest of his life. We heard from a neurologist who came to Station One that, in his opinion, these injuries often would present challenges and symptoms like Jim was experiencing for up to a year. The Doc explained that mental functions would come back over the next year and not to give up hope and our support for Jim and his family.

About 6 months after the fire and his injuries, Jim, with the aid of a cane and department friends, as able to walk with assistance into Station One to say hello to everybody. Several off-duty firefighters and his wife accompanied him. We all looked forward to once again sharing coffee with Jim.

Jim went on to thank everybody in broken sentences. Jim's thank you was unnecessary. He was and will always be a firefighter family member. Jim spoke in broken sentences with great difficulty keeping sentences understandable. Jim also asked for more clarity about what happened to him at the YMCA fire.

Jim also told the crew about his struggles with memory. His wife confirmed the memory difficulties, even simple things such as his wife's and children's names. She went on to explain little things like going to a store were difficult for him, and putting things down around the house and not remembering where they were, presented challenges for Jim.

What we shared that day with Jim and his wife shouldn't have happened to Jim. He was once a beautiful spirit firefighter with a massive presence in this department, wherever he was. It was easy to feel upset and pissed off that somebody we didn't know could fall asleep smoking and drinking in bed, and this tragedy would happen to Jim. The concern for Jim was palpable by all the firefighters on duty that day. Jim was never going to return to the job he loved. He would never again be able to throw nuts and bolts under Ken's Engine 1. The department and community had lost a very talented and dedicated firefighter. Forever.

Jim was well cared for by the City and the state through their many firefighter benefit programs. The benefits programs were established throughout the state to assist firefighters injured in the line of duty. But, the bottom line was that Jim was a very young man in his early thirties whose life was now changed forever. Jim would face many more challenges in the future. Jim and his family also faced that at least half of Jim's life would involve mental and physical struggles. The department and local and state taxpayers would incur tremendous financial costs, and it would be in the millions of dollars.

Over the next year or so, Jim stopped two or three times to Station One with his family and wife to provide periodic updates. So, again, to also remember a time past, but even more importantly, to remember that he was and will always be a part of our firefighting family. He was a forever member of the family of firefighters, and his firefighting family cared for him.

Over the following years, there were many things Jim would require to make life easier for himself and his family. He needed ramps for his home's outside entrances, a new roof, a remodeled kitchen, a first-floor bedroom, and a list of other projects. Jim could count on the men and women of our fire department to be there whenever needed.

And then there were those firefighters who just stopped by his house to share a story, discuss life in general or take Jim fishing. Fishing and golf became his favorite things to do. The distance between Jim and the department would grow wider as the years passed. Sadly, his wife eventually divorced Jim. His permanent injuries, mental disabilities, and physical restrictions might have been factors in the outcome of this story. I don't know for sure.

Although limited in the sport of golf, Jim reportedly loved doing what he could do on a course. Jim, in time, moved back to his rural hometown to be closer to other family members. By his doing so, we finally lost touch with Jim.

Jim did pass away doing what he loved, playing golf and fishing with his three brothers. He was in his early 50s when he passed. One cannot help but think that Jim might have lived a fuller life without the permanent physical and mental injuries he received one night on the third floor of the YMCA. Jim may not have crossed his fine red line at the YMCA, but he would live next to it for years to come trying to manage the challenges of his permanent fire ground injuries.

Firefighting presents a broad range and severity of life-threatening dangers. Whether at the emergency scene, on the way to or from an emergency, or while simply training, volunteer and career firefighters suffer permanent injury and death far too often. Each year, tens of thousands of firefighters are injured while fighting fires, rescuing people, responding to emergency medical and hazardous material incidents, or training for their jobs. These types of career-ending injuries exact great financial and personal losses on the fire service and the communities these men and women serve as firefighters. And let us not forget the tragic impacts on their families and loved ones. Divorce is all too common in these situations.

"When a man or woman becomes a firefighter, their greatest act of bravery has been accomplished. What they do after that is all in the line of duty."

– Edward Croker

CHAPTER 5

LIFE TOOLS FROM RECRUIT SCHOOL AND ROOKIE LIFE

My father called about 1:30 p.m. on a sunny afternoon while I was working at my part-time job as a community camp counselor. He said the executive secretary to the department's Fire Chief had called the house looking for me. I wondered why they were calling, having waited so long to hear anything from the Fire Department I was trying to get hired by. I was certainly anxious to hear what the call was about.

The quest to become a firefighter paramedic began 2 years earlier after joining two volunteer fire departments and watching the television show *Emergency*. The two main characters in that show, Gage and DeSoto, seemed to have an occupation and internal calling, which was both exciting and more in line with my physical abilities than my mental abilities. In addition, I hadn't done very well at the university, as grades and attendance were more important to them than me.

My first steps for earning a position with a professional career fire department had begun 6 months earlier with an application to the fire department and a request to become a member of their 1974 Recruit Class. Finally, after struggling in college and 2 plus years as a member and working with two separate volunteer departments in the area, I hoped to hear some good news.

Rumors at the time were that the department would hire as many as fifty new firefighters for their newest recruit class as career firefighters. The first milestone to being hired would be the department's written exam. They held the exam in a local high school, where each room could accommodate about seventy-five individuals testing at a time. There were approximately 1,000 applicants for these fifty positions, with the chosen recruits to begin training in August of the year. The written exam was about 3 hours long, and I was excited to hear later I had achieved a passing grade. After successfully passing the first hurdle, the next hurdle would be the physical exam.

The location for the physical exam was the University Campus Athletic Facilities. Approximately ten firefighting-related physical challenges were evaluated for testing each of the remaining five hundred applicants who had passed the written exam. Some challenges had strict time requirements, and some required the applicant just to achieve and prove they could complete the specific challenge Testing covered back muscles, arm strength, leg muscles, and just about any other muscle needed for the demands of firefighting. The most difficult part of the exam for me was to climb the 50-foot rope to the ceiling.

The physical exam concluded with a one-mile run under very strict times. Firefighters from across the fire department held stopwatches on individual runners as the run occurred. We ran in groups of a dozen or so. About one hundred individuals passed the written and physical exams. Those individuals who passed both were then invited to an oral interview.

The Oral Interview Panel consisted of an Assistant Chief of the Fire Department and several citizens. One of the citizen interviewers was a local elementary school principal I knew, but I didn't recognize the others. I knew her because she had been my elementary school principal many years prior. They asked their five predetermined questions and jotted notes as the candidates answered. Concluding the interview, they said, "Thanks for applying to be a firefighter." Then the waiting began. The wait was 2-3 months before my father received the call saying I had been hired. I was excited to hear the news after all of the testing, I had placed fifth in the New Recruit Class of fifty hired by the department. My dream came true.

The #5 hiring position would stand as my seniority designation throughout the rest of my departmental career. This position would be my first introduction to the professional career of fire service. After a couple of years of volunteering with smaller area town departments, and at 20 years of age, I joined the 1974 Recruit Class. We were all given 3 weeks to report to the Fire Department's Training Facility.

On August 4, 1974, this volunteer firefighter joined forty-nine others to take the first steps to become a career firefighter. The first step in our training was to go to a local hospital where all fifty recruits would be given physical exams by a team of medical students from the university's medical school. The medical exam results would confirm whether you were healthy enough to be officially sworn in as a firefighter. I aced it, and I was then sworn in as a firefighter. Little did I realize it then, but I was also joining a new family of firefighters throughout the state and nation.

Being my first real career job of any kind, I didn't think the medical exam was difficult or serious. At least not until the training officers pulled one applicant out of the class and informed him that he was no longer considered for the firefighter position and asked to leave the training facility.

It was explained to us by the department training officers this individual suffered from asthma. Asthma could lead to severe breathing difficulties in very hazardous conditions. According to the department, the applicant was excused from the Training Academy. The following day, the next successful applicant on the list, apparently #51, was added to the class to maintain the recruit class number at 50. We were measured for uniforms and given old helmets, boots, and turn-out gear for use while our new turn-out gear was made to measure.

Some early training involved the fire department's 100-foot aerial ladder. The vehicle was in rough shape and had a right twist in the last section of the ladder. As one climbed to the top of the ladder, it would roll to the right, making it very scary to go to the top. It wasn't bad at 50 feet, but it felt you were almost sideways at 100 feet in the air. The training officers quickly wanted to determine whether you feared heights, which would have been another reason for excusing you from the training facility. The climb was challenging because it was also a freestanding ladder. The ladder twisted and bounced up and down unless it leaned against a building or some other solid structure to stabilize it.

A couple of the recruits were nervous starting up the ladder but could climb the first challenge of 50 feet. Not being afraid of heights, climbing to 50 feet didn't bother me, although the twist did. In subsequent days the height would increase to 75 and then finally to 100 feet in the air. At the top of the ladder was a bell that the department training staff had attached. The Staff asked all recruits to "simply" climb the 100 feet and ring the bell.

Other challenges in training were for getting used to and working in smoke. The burn building was an old military building that allowed the training Staff to set different kinds of fires and create differing scenarios. Some fires were to experience smoke. Other fires were to experience the heat and smoke that a burning structure generates. At one point, they requested we remove our masks and stay in the smoke-filled building as long as possible. I don't know how long I lasted. I wasn't the last recruit to leave the building, but I wasn't the first one out, either. It was horrible. It hurt, it stunk, and it burned. This challenge wasn't a pleasant experience, and in today's volunteer and career training standards, this method of smoke training wouldn't be acceptable as a training challenge. Breathing any smoke is unacceptable.

At one point during our 4 weeks of training, the Fire Department was able to secure a center city house scheduled for demolition. So, we participated in many real-life challenges in the old building for 2 days. We cut a lot of holes. We pulled apart a lot of ceilings. But, most important was the opportunity to use all of the department's saws and hand-tool equipment.

The following recruit class, 4 years later, was also able to find an old abandoned house for training. Unlike our class, the training staff had planned a series of scenarios involving setting live fires. The recruits were assembled and assigned their given tasks. The first fire was set in a second-floor bedroom using pallets. As a result, the house burned down when the fire got away from the training staff. This situation was one of those times when you had to shake your head and giggle.

Returning to the story of my training class. When my fellow recruits and I started in the Fire Department, it was rare for firefighters to use breathing apparatus (SCBAs) at any time. A breathing apparatus was only to be used for exceptional circumstances, and those firefighters who wore SCBAs were considered "weak." Another derogative word was frequently used regarding those who wore SCBAs. We were the first firefighting recruit class required to wear masks at all fires, including car fires.

At that time, we spent 90% of our training time on fire ground operations and fire suppression activities. We dedicated no time to fire prevention or fire protection equipment like sprinkler systems and standpipes. Instead, the training was all about putting fires out and surviving in the station culture.

We went by bus to a nearby YMCA sometime in the middle of our training. The final hurdle for becoming a permanent firefighter was to swim the length of the Olympic pool. To demonstrate "no fear of water," and to be able to swim

50 meters. Everyone passed with one exception. One recruit firefighter had to retake the test for failing to stay in his lane. He had gone three-quarters of the 50 meters and somehow got completely turned around in the water, returning to where he had started. He had probably gone twice the distance required, just not in a straight line. He would eventually pass. We all knew this was the final physical hurdle. With excitement, we awaited our station and shift assignments.

Having finished the evaluated training and written exams held throughout the 4 weeks of training, I finished fifth in my class of fifty. For doing so well, I thought my assignment would be to any one of the busy downtown stations, especially Station One the busiest firehouse in the city. But, instead, the higher you finished in the recruit class training, the further you were assigned away from the busy daily fire action. I was honored to join the department ranks but saddened to find out I was now assigned to the station furthest away from the action in the city. My first station was known as the fire department's "Country Club" and "Rest Home."

I turned 21 on my first day in Station 5, and the second closest individual to my age was Eddy, a 50-year-old single guy and a true goofball. The remaining six firefighters and officers were also in their 50s and nearing the mandatory retirement age of 55. There was one firefighter just under 50 years old (maybe 49), Robert, but he was such a miserable son of a bitch no other station wanted him.

Being the Shift Rookie, my days were spent cleaning equipment, cleaning various station areas, and refinishing the damn wooden chairs. (Bad memories resurfacing thinking of those damn chairs.) The station's officers had decided the new rookies on the three shifts would sand, refinish, and varnish the two dozen or so hundred-year-old wooden chairs found around the station. Mindless waste of time.

While doing busy work, the others had ping pong, croquette, archery, and softball pitch and catch to fill their days. Calls for response? No, not really. Being on the city's edge, and working with the crew of misfit toys, we were surrounded by all new homes, rural properties, and new businesses. While the City Center Stations were toning out throughout the day and night, our station's fire vehicles ran an average of three emergency calls per day. The Engine I was assigned to might get one or two calls a week, usually for a car accident, but primarily to assist our Medics with lifting a patient. Only our Medic Unit 5 remained quite busy.

Sitting here, I cannot remember the Ladder Company ever being called out even once in my first 3 months there. But, thank heavens, had they been called out, we would have spent 10 critical minutes removing the bird nests, bats and dust from around the wheels.

While my youthfulness and desire to see action were undoubtedly high, it was easy to see why these individuals had assignments to such a quiet station. Firefighting is a very high-stress and very physical occupation. Yet, these individuals had certainly done their time and served with honor in the busiest stations of the city.

The invaluable information, experiences, and education gained through these individuals served me well in my career. I learned how to "really" set ladders, manage charged hose lines through a burning house, and use different tools when searching for fire victims. I learned what equipment to carry in my turn-out gear pockets at all times.

For an example of this unique practical recommendation, one station firefighter had developed a simple but very effective tool for keeping doors open and unlocked. The tool was simply cut from rubber innertubes in the shape of a figure 8. The Figure 8 was placed on the outside door latch of the room as you entered through the door and then by stretching the other loop over the internal latch and placing it over the opposite side doorknob. In summary, this prevented a door you've crawled through in a burning building from closing and latching behind you, preventing your escape and possibly leading to personal injury or even a firefighter's death.

In every station in the United States, there are different pieces of equipment firefighters have invented or made themselves to protect themselves and their fellow firefighters. When I left the job 21 years later, I still carried some of these homemade tools in my fire coat pockets. Including the 6 years behind a desk, I carried these and several similar tools in a pair of rarely worn turn-out gear.

Within a year after this first assignment to Station 5, I was invited by the department to become a paramedic. At the age of 21, I began 9 months of training at the local medical school. Years later, while speaking in Los Angeles, I had the opportunity to visit the LA County Museum and sit in Squad 51 from the show *Emergency*. I later met actor Randy Mantooth who played firefighter/paramedic John Gage. The crazy circles of life.

“The only thing stronger than a firefighter is the bond between firefighters.”

-Unknown

CHAPTER 6

HOW QUICKLY LIFE CHANGES

It was a new Spring weekend morning, so full of life, warm with the awakening sounds of the season. Station 5's shift started at its usual time, 7 am with morning radio checks. We then checked emergency equipment on the vehicles for the day, and then the firefighters were ready for our first coffee break, complete with peanut butter toast. It was a Monday morning, and most Mondays were typically quiet days for the station personnel and the department across the city. The morning coffee always was the place to catch up on weekend activities and, as always, to solve the world's problems.

Several firefighters played golf over the past weekend, as the city courses had just opened, and they shared several tall tales. Other firefighters had attended various weekend outdoor events in the area. One firefighter, Jan, shared the arrival of a new horse at her barn, and yes, we even had one firefighter who slept through coffee. Single, of course. Tough weekend, no doubt. Others had children at home, and their weekends were simple—a lot of soccer games and a lot of driving from one field or activity to another.

One of the life updates of most interest at the table this particular morning, Firefighters Phil and Joe had secured their fishing licenses for the rapidly approaching fishing season. The start of Musky season was just a short 2 weeks away, and getting lake reports was of interest to the entire crew. We were fortunate to have been in an area of Musky habitat and some of the best Musky fishing in the country.

As a crew, we all enjoyed anytime we could get out on the area lakes. With soccer, horses, football, and driving to our horse stable, I valued most my boating time on the lakes fishing for Musky. Unfortunately, as my four children grew older, my time on the area lakes grew shorter and shorter each year. Firefighter Joe was a nationally, well-known fishing guide; so anything he said was a golden fishing tip.

Both Phil and Joe were avid outdoors individuals. They hunted, trapped, and fished together. Both firefighters were well-known for their outdoor knowledge and skills.

On this day, a new lieutenant, Charlie, was filling in for the day, as the station's permanent Engine company officer was away on vacation. As a new lieutenant, he had come to the station that day bearing gifts.

He spent his weekend hunting ducks. It seemed like a strange time of the year to be hunting ducks. We never did determine if he owned the land he was hunting out of season on. Most likely, these were freezer ducks. Having sat in his freezer for over a year, he or his wife thought taking them to the fire station would be an excellent way to get rid of them.

Over the years, many firefighters graciously brought in the fruits of their hunting and fishing trips. Of course, we all appreciated their offerings. Deer and lake trout, and salmon were the most common. However, a real delicacy was Smelt. At least once or twice a year, the crew could count on a station dinner of Smelt, French fries, and Coleslaw. Some bear chops on rare occasions and even elk steaks, but...back to the ducks.

Dick was our cook that day and was the best of us cooking. So having duck done by Dick was worth looking forward to. Hence the great debate that began with morning coffee. Lt. Charlie had brought in six thawed ducks. He was adamant the ducks be placed in a 500-degree preheated oven, left there to cook for an hour, and then with the range turned off, the ducks were to cool for another couple hours slowly. Lt. Charlie said this was his family's recipe, and this method would cook the ducks perfectly. Dick insisted this was no way to cook duck and that after the 3 hours of oven time at those requested temperatures would destroy the meat.

The cooks then made a decision. Three of the ducks would be placed in the inferno oven of 500 degrees, while Dick would cook the remaining three ducks his way in a second oven. Dick's temp was 350 degrees and involved considerable basting. The crew would taste and compare the six ducks at lunch. Loser to buy ice cream with toppings for the crew.

At the 3-hour mark, the crew gathered around to see which cook had won ice cream for the station. Dick's ducks came out first from his oven. They were a beautiful golden brown with crispy skin, juicy, and just wonderful. Lt. Charlie pulled out of the other oven his ducks made with his family recipe. Holy crap. The first thing was the color. I wonder if any paint companies had that color on their pallets. After that, the fat from the duck was burned to the bottom of the pan, which probably explained why the kitchen smelled funky during the cookoff.

There was also a strange metallic substance on Lt. Charlie's ducks. As best we could tell, the oven was hot enough to melt the lead shot out of the duck. That meant warnings went out for the firefighters to be careful with the lieutenant's ducks, as they also contained lead shot in the meat. In addition, Lt. Charlie's ducks and family recipe caused the ducks to become like basketballs. So funky were the Charlie's cooked ducks; I suspect you could have dribbled them, for you surely couldn't cut into them without an effort. Bet settled. Dick was our cook and clear winner, and Lt. Charlie would have to go to the grocery store for the crew's ice cream treats.

It was a beautiful spring day. The 9:00 am coffee also included a crew member's birthday over the past weekend. When a birthday occurs, it's customary for the firefighter who had the birthday to bring in donuts or cake for the firefighters on duty. A special treat indeed. I would never figure out how this tradition began. But if you had a birthday, you owed your crew a sweet treat in celebration on your first shift back.

We completed all of the coffee and birthday sweets, and we were off to make our beds for the shift and begin the station work of cleaning and washing and drying the dirty hoses and equipment from weekend fires. Washing and hanging 50-foot sections of hose to dry in the hose tower was very labor intensive. But it was Monday, and Mondays typically provided quiet periods without many emergency calls.

Around 1:30 pm, tones suddenly opened and sounded aloud throughout the station.

"Attention Engine 5, 888 Kohler Mills Road, for a report of a vehicle fire. Time out 1330."

Engine 5 was dispatched to a reported car fire in a driveway against a residential structure, presumably a house or garage. The address of the emergency was just a short distance from the station. Dispatchers also added in the dispatch the 911 caller was reporting flames and smoke visible coming from the front compartment of an older model pickup truck he was refinishing. As the Engine crew loaded up and moved out of the station with lights and sirens, it gave the rest of the crew time to prepare for our building fire inspections that coming afternoon.

It wasn't but 10-15 minutes when the tones again broke the silence throughout the station—this time, they sounded for our medic unit to respond to the same location as the car fire our Engine just responded to.

"Attention Medic 5, respond to 888 Kohler Mill Road for an injured firefighter. Time out 1347."

The report was clearly for a traumatic injury involving one of our crew members from Engine 5. Unknown who the firefighter was at the time of dispatch.

As I write this, I suspect most don't realize how dangerous car fires are. Yes, one can perceive flame and smoke as problematic, but what's in the smoke when a car burn is incredibly deadly; things can explode such as gasoline and now lithium batteries, and I could go on with my car fire warnings. In addition, there are all kinds of harmful, cancer-causing chemicals from burning cars with the many plastic components now in all vehicles.

As we responded to the address of the fire, there were no other details provided except we could hear our Lt. Charlie, the visiting company officer on the Engine radio system, asking for the ambulance to **"STEP IT UP."** By saying, "step it up," the officer is really saying, "hurry, I need you here NOW." We understood well the urgency of the lieutenant's voice. My partner that day Bob and I did what we could to hurry.

I have difficulty describing this chaotic scene as we pulled onto the location. We found the vehicle, which had been burning atop in the driveway, was now down the driveway, against the Engine. Strangely, a firefighter lay in the grass and being attended to by two other crew members, including the lieutenant, while another firefighter was still dousing the truck fire with water. Fortunately, the truck fire was out. Let me just say it, there was blood everywhere.

As the Engine pump operator, Phil was apparently positioned at the Engine's pump panel to ensure firefighters had a water supply at proper pressures. Unfortunately, during the firefighting of the vehicle fire, the brakes on the burning truck failed and released. The fire had severed the brake lines. As a result, on an elevated driveway leading to the garage, the vehicle had rolled down the driveway directly toward the Engine and Phil. With the sound of the Engine pumping water with its diesel motor running on high, Phil clearly couldn't hear calls from the other firefighters above at the vehicle to get out of the way as the truck rolled down the driveway directly toward Phil.

Running under the Engine's pump panel is a diamond plated step. These are referred to in the fire service as "running boards." These running boards are approximately

18-24 inches from the ground and serve several purposes for firefighters working on and around these large vehicles.

While Phil stood watching his pump gauges, with his back to the fire, the now moving vehicle began rolling down the driveway. As it would happen, the truck's back bumper was approximately a little over 2 feet off the ground. In an instant, a nano second of time, the rear bumper of the burning truck contacted Engine 5 and Phil. The back bumper of the truck fit exactly above the running board. This series of events instantly created the same effect as a pair of scissors when the truck and Engine 5 came together at the pump panel. There couldn't have been more than an inch difference in height between the Engine's running board and the bumper of the truck.

While Phil was standing at the panel with his left leg perched resting on the running board his right leg was on the ground, the impact of the two vehicles partially severed Phil's right leg. The two vehicles came together as they did, like scissors crushing bone and partially severing Phil's right lower leg at the knee or just above. We couldn't tell for sure. As a result, Phil's leg was almost 60% amputated at or just above his right knee.

Fortunately, Paul, a fill-in (detailed) firefighter/ paramedic on Engine 5 that day immediately tended to Phil's partial amputation. Paul immediately placed tourniquets on Phil to stop the bleeding. As we arrived on location, we successfully established IV lines of lactated ringers. One IV was in each arm, and Paul continued to work on stopping the bleeding. I credit Paul with saving Phil's life. Phil may have bled out if Paul had not been there and known what to do.

How could this be? Just an hour before, the crew was laughing about cooked ducks and the upcoming fishing season.

We wasted absolutely no time with Phil. The crew quickly loaded Phil into the ambulance for the race to the City's Level One Trauma Medical Center. Phil was conscious and talking the entire trip to the Trauma Center. He realized he had significant leg damage. Our haste and facial expressions probably concerned him more. We hadn't done much with his right leg. We had cut away his pants and could see the skin and some remaining muscle and tendons still attached to the leg. I can't imagine what he felt seeing his leg partially wrapped, covered in blood, and our haste to stop bleeding.

We continued to race toward the trauma center, advising the medical team by radio that surgeons would need to be on standby for Phil upon our arrival and to the severe extent of the injuries we had been dealing with. It would be about a 15-20-minute ride to the Medical Center at a high rate of speed. It seemed tragic that we bypassed two other hospitals on the way. But the Trauma Center was where Phil needed to go.

However, Phil was our firefighting crew mate, and we determined these other medical facilities would have been unable to quickly assemble the necessary surgical teams needed for Phil and this leg trauma.

Once we arrived at the Trauma Center, we were led quickly to one of the emergency room suites. Phil wasn't there long before he was ultimately taken upstairs for X-Ray and the surgical area for the further examination leading to surgery in an attempt to save his right leg. I could never say enough about the medical professionals in this nation who have to deal with these kinds of traumatic injuries. They just seem to know injured firefighters are doing their duties to protect the city and all docs and nurses work hard to ensure their survival and they receive first-class care.

It's incredible to witness the efforts put into downed first responders, in this case, Phil. As a fire department employee, our firefighting crew went from a beautiful spring day coffee filled with stories, a duck cooking contest, coffee, and just goodwill among firefighters to one of our very own now being very tragically injured.

Phil was in our thoughts the rest of the shift and beyond, and we took every opportunity to follow Phil's medical journey closely throughout the day. How can these things happen? Why did these things happen to firefighters? And in reality, the accident victim could have been any one of us? Such a fine line between perfect health and permanent life changes and challenges.

Administrative department chiefs and other medic units visited Phil and extended their good wishes to him. The outpouring from strangers witnessed some very considerate and beautiful things happening at the station. Many from the surrounding station neighborhoods dropped off cards and even some stuffed animals. But, we never heard a fucking word from the guy who had the truck fire. Jerk.

Unfortunately, given the injury caused by the burning truck that crushed his leg, blood loss, and the time it took us to get him to a Medical Center, the surgeons decided it was impossible to save Phil's leg. So while I'm sure there would be much rehabilitation and a great effort into helping Phil over time, this injury would change the quality of this remarkable individual's life forever. Yet, surprisingly, Phil never lost a moment in deciding to get on with life. Phil quickly pointed out he could now fish every day.

The shocking reality for the department members was that this young, energetic outdoor vibrant firefighter was full of life, single, and always a source of a great smile if you needed one. But, unfortunately, Phil would no longer have a firefighting career. In just one instant, the truck bumper fitting exactly over the diamond plating of Phil's Engine 5 altered his life irretrievably.

Again, another fine red line crossed between work and a firefighting career. In a nano-second, Phil faced a life of rehab and challenges with one leg missing. Had the truck been 2 inches higher or lower, would this have been the same outcome for Phil? I can't say.

With the greatest admiration and traditions of all department firefighters, Phil refused to let this tragic accident deter him. He was a Viet Nam veteran with a heart of gold and a fighting spirit that was as tough as nails. By department policy, Phil was given an opportunity for a full medical disability and retirement, which included future training for other employment options. But his firefighting days were done.

Phil accepted his medical disability and retirement, and a true loss to the department. However, due to his love of service to others and his love of the community, Phil would help others with similar disabilities as his, enjoy the outdoors through hunting, fishing, and bird watching. According to friends and family, Phil also took up painting, where he got pretty good apparently. Unfortunately, he passed away at a much too young age, in his early 50s. I hope it wasn't from the traumatic injury he had suffered during his experience with the fine line between life and death. Phil never lost his smile, nor did we ever forget that smile.

Volunteer and career firefighters report an average of over 75,000 injuries yearly from fire responses. A quarter of these, like Phil, result in lost time or complete career-ending disabilities. Career firefighters have little to worry about if disabled. Volunteers, however, are in a much different situation. Volunteers risk losing their very livelihoods if disabled in service to their communities. Volunteers come from all walks of life. Many serve their fellow residents without any guarantee that they'll be cared for should they become permanently disabled.

Firefighters know the fine red line and face it all too often.

"A firefighter's job is to save lives and protect property, but their passion is to serve."

-Unknown

CHAPTER 7

HOMECOMING HORROR

Our annual University Homecoming is a very important day on campus and in the downtown area of the city. Our Fire Station One commonly runs twenty to thirty calls in 24 hours on a homecoming day. Coming on the shift in the morning, the city firefighters knew it would be a busy day with a wide variety of calls. Specifically, the four downtown area stations, particularly the Medic Units, would be very busy. From serious life-threatening emergencies to minor emergencies in our local drinking establishments, it would be a busy day. With beautiful, brisk fall weather and clear skies, you could feel it would be busy. Little did we know just how busy.

The university had a long-standing tradition of exciting parties on campus during homecoming week, particularly in the five-block area of numerous university Greek Society Frats and Sororities. From outdoor toga parties to costume parties, there was no shortage of locations or reasons to consume alcoholic beverages. Adding to these parties was the students' enjoyment of pulling box alarms (false alarms). It was to be a busy day.

On this day, it had been as busy as I and my partner Steve had expected. With some heart and breathing issues mixed with traumatic injuries from falls and trips, most requests for paramedics were alcohol-related. Falling, fighting, and a patient suffering from hypothermia at the stadium would make for a busy day of service. The hypothermia patient we suspect resulted from going bare-chested in forty-degree weather with not enough antifreeze in his system.

Station One had finally calmed down for a while around bar closing time. The Engine Company slowed after a day of false alarms, automatic alarms, and an endless night of trash fires. These were common after a football victory. (They were common after all home games, whom am I kidding?)

A good feeling comes over Station One when calm, a wonderful quiet, plays against the history of being the busiest station in the city. Constant runs in and out, equipment cleaning, and training all take a moment of reflection and remembrance to all who have served from Station One and the history they carried with them. It was close to 2 am, and while most firefighters opted to drink coffee and discuss topics of anyone's choice, others debated whether to risk grabbing a few minutes of sleep in the remaining 5 hours of the shift. Finally, the silence of the city's fire stations was pierced at 2:04 am by the tone out of the 911 Center.

"Attention Engine 3, Engine 4, Truck 8 and One Complete, fire reported by several phone calls at 408 College Court. This address is the Sigma Chi Fraternity

building. Students are reported to be trapped inside. Time out 2:05."

There was a time in the past when dispatch toned out city-wide stations with a loud shrill. Department administration believed the tone had to be loud enough to awaken even the unconscious sleeping firefighter. Imagine hearing something so loud and piercing as to make firefighters literally jump out of their beds. Imagine the damage to a firefighter's cardiac system being abruptly woken up from a sound sleep into the resulting massive adrenaline dump. One can only wonder what the damage is to the body's systems when startled out of sleep like this several times a night.

Although there are eleven fire stations in the city, if dispatch announces a fire, there was a time 911 toned out in all the fire stations, regardless of emergency location. This practice dates back to the beginning of the fire department when all firefighters could be called to a fire. Unfortunately, the department's cultural belief at the time of this fire was if one had a fire, all stations had a fire. Therefore, you could be toned out three times a night for fires on the opposite side of the city, with no chance of you ever being called to assist. Imagine the damage done to firefighters' bodies by sounding these tones throughout all departments in the city. I can only wonder what impact this had on a firefighter's immune system.

So concerned was our departmental Medical Director about this dispatching practice and the possible resulting cardio-vascular damage, he requested the 911 Comms Center eventually drop the loud tones and install (actually by duct tape) a doorbell to the dispatch boards. Soft and enough of a station alert with two simple "ding dongs."

"For units responding to College Courts, we are receiving numerous reports seeing flames on the top floor and roof, occupants are evacuating.

The typical response to a first alarm assignment as mentioned earlier would dispatch two Engine Companies, a Ladder Company, a Medic Unit, and a Battalion Chief. That should bring a minimum of seventeen firefighters on the first due fire assignment, as the National Fire Protection Association (NFPA) guidelines recommended. A second alarm would duplicate the first alarm with another seventeen firefighters, and a third alarm would duplicate the first and second alarms with another seventeen firefighters. After a third alarm, our city was drained of fire protection. Unlike the bigger Metropolitan cities, three alarms was our limit. Therefore every request for another fire department resource would have to be specifically identified for those units to respond. Once over three alarms, our city would also bring in volunteer fire departments to city stations in order to help cover the city.

Men and women volunteer firefighters brought into the city to assist fire protection bring with them the same dedication as career firefighters. But, unfortunately, our city wasn't as resource-rich as the large metropolitan fire departments.

In a full-alarm response, as was the case this homecoming night, Ladder 1 (once called a Hook and Ladder) would go first, followed by Engine 1 (Sometimes called a Pumper). Medic Unit One trailed behind these two large fire apparatuses, followed by the Battalion Chief with their driver or aide. The ladder company would always go first due to the size and need for space for such a large vehicle. In addition, once parked on the fire scene, Ladder companies are very difficult to move, whereas Engines and Medic Units are smaller, required less space, and were more versatile and easier to relocate if necessary.

Ladder Company One required two drivers. One up front for the cab and a second driver perched high on the aerial ladders directly over the rear wheels. In the fire service, this position is called the "Tiller Position."

Due to the length of the ladder company, the up-front driver would focus on controlling the cab and turning corners, while the Tiller driver in control of the rear wheels kept the wheels straight and, once clear of the sides or length of the ladders, would in turn then make the turn around the same corner. This maneuver allowed the large Ladder Company to make tight turns when driven in harmony between the front and back (Tiller).

We were among large multistory and some very old buildings as soon as Station One entered the College Court area. Steve and I could see the glow of the fire in the night sky. We could also smell the smoke of a structure fire. It's a very distinctive smell. And clearly a large fire.

As this was the center of so many homecoming parties, one couldn't miss the large number of illegally parked cars haphazardly parked on both sides of the area's narrow streets. College Court was packed with illegally parked cars. The fire building was at the end of College Court, which was a cul-de-sac with only one narrow way in.

This fire building location required fire trucks to make a very tight right-hand turn onto a very small side street. This first right-hand turn for the Ladder Company onto Henry Street was a challenge created by several large Frats and Sororities guarding the entrance. This first tight right turn would be followed by another VERY sharp right turn directly onto College Court, a very small alleyway leading to the burning building. The distance between the entrance onto College Court from Henry Street and the burning structure was about 75 yards down a narrow alley. College Court was only approximately 40 feet wide.

On this night, however, with cars illegally parked randomly everywhere you looked, the first right-hand turn onto Henry Street became next to impossible. This first turn was an extremely tight turn for the Ladder and Tiller and bit less of a tight turn for the fire vehicles following behind. Engine 1, Medic 1, and BC One were now completely stopped from moving forward, awaiting Ladder 1 to navigate this first turn onto Henry Street. Finally, Ladder 1 was able to slowly make it around the corner onto Henry Street.

The next right-hand turn into College Court from Henry was much tighter for the Ladder Company to make. The cab could make it barely, but it left the Tiller driver in an impossible position to guide the rear of Ladder 1 around the College Court corner. Our shift had the best tiller driver in the city. It was frustrating to have all responding fire units stuck on Henry Street, 200 yards from the growing fire, and with no way to proceed until the Ladder Company safely got around this final turn into the College Court alley.

As if on cue, bystanders began yelling and attempting to get the attention of arriving firefighters to the building and toward the top floor. The top floor was the attic. The attic had a bunch of dormer windows for light and summertime ventilation. Looking ahead of Ladder 1, a young man in one of the attic windows was screaming "FIRE" and "HELP ME PLEASE" and trying to get the attention of everyone in the immediate area, especially firefighters 75 yards away temporarily stuck at the alley entrance.

Some 200 bystanders had gathered in and around the alley way drawn by the noises of victims and fire trucks. Unfortunately, many bystanders were inebriated from all the homecoming activities. Sadly, half of those present yelled "JUMP" to the young man standing in the dormer opening while other bystanders yelled, "DON'T JUMP!"

No one can begin to imagine what this young man was facing in the upper attic with flame and smoke growing around him. It's difficult to remember my confusion and growing concern with so many people pleading with firefighters to hurry. Most of the people who were yelling and pointing were very drunk. One can only imagine the conditions in that attic with the fire burning throughout the walls of the building below. The smoke. The inability to breathe. The immense heat. The screaming outside.

As my Station One fellow firefighters saw the young man in the window, and understood the growing fire conditions, and witnessed the actions of bystanders, it became very clear the log jam of fire vehicles created by illegally parked cars had to be freed. It had to be cleared, and RIGHT NOW! If this young man was to survive, we needed to get much closer.

At this moment, Ladder Company One Lieutenant Robert decided to order the Ladder to move forward regardless of the vehicles blocking the intersection. (Robert was the best fire officer I ever knew or worked for.) As Robert ordered the Ladder 1 to move forward slowly, one could suddenly hear the sounds of metal, plastic, and glass crunching and shattering. As one expected, we firefighters witnessed the side of the Ladder Company crawl over, crunch, bang, and scrape those cars illegally parked along the alley. The decision made by Lt. Robert was quick and simply the right thing to do. Perfect.

The rear wheels of Ladder 1 climbed over a small foreign car, first crushing the car's passenger and engine compartments. Next up was the rear wheels over the car's trunk area and then slam down to the pavement. Ladder 1 had completely crushed the car. Next up was another small car where the rear wheels of the Ladder Company climbed up onto the engine compartment of the second car, crushing the front of the car including the driver's compartment area. Then the passenger side quarter panel and door. As amazing as it was to witness, the rear of Ladder 1 was now once again on the pavement of College Court, clear of the illegally parked vehicles and slowly moving toward the fire building.

The log jam was now resolved, and all fire department units could navigate the tight turn by being smaller in size. A voice was heard on the radio for the following responding large fire vehicles to hold short up on the main thoroughfare until it was determined if more Ladder Companies were needed.

The tiller driver would later tell us about looking down through the ladders and watching the rear wheels go up the hood of a vehicle, over two roofs of several others, and even though the passenger area of one vehicle. These cars were parked illegally, and Lt Robert decided the priority was to get to the young college student on the upper floor. In doing so, I would guess four to five cars were damaged, anywhere from a few bad scrapes to the total destruction of vehicles. I've always wondered how surprised the parents and owners of these crushed vehicles felt when they learned their cars were driven over by a very large fire vehicle.

A fire hydrant was at the corner of the alley leading to the fire building. Fortunately, the hydrant was one of the only things still left undamaged by the Ladder Company's car crushing actions. This hydrant allowed securing a water supply very convenient for Engine 1. The Engine 1 Captain ordered a crew member to drop one 5-inch supply hose and one 2½-inch supply line at the hydrant. He further requested Steve and me on Medic 1 to "make the hydrant." This order was fire speak for us to hook up the hose to the hydrant and standby to turn the hydrant water flow on for the pump operator of Engine 1.

As instructed, the two supply lines were looped around the hydrant, and a hydrant wrench was dropped on the ground next to the hydrant. Steve and I removed the hydrant caps and attached the two supply lines. All that was left to complete our assigned task was get a signal from the Engine 1 driver for the hydrant valve to be opened and water to flow. The Engine Company pump operator signaled Steve and me with two blasts from the horn on Engine 1. Twenty-six turns of the nut atop the hydrant with our hydrant wrench later, and water was freely flowing to Engine Company One.

As the Engine 1 operator moved quickly to attach a supply line to the pump, the Engine Company Captain and a firefighter grabbed a 1.5-inch preconnected attack hose line. They entered the fire building, trying to get water quickly on this rapidly growing fire. The outside firefighters from Ladder 1 and Engine 4 reassured the occupant in the attic window to stay put and not to jump.

As the water supply was being secured to the Engine and a hose line being advanced from Engine 1, the firefighters and Lieutenant Robert from the Ladder company began to hydraulically raise the 100-foot aerial ladder to the young man in the attic dormer window. It takes only moments to safely raise such a large ladder. Stabilizers go down. Wheels secured from rolling. And firefighters dressed in safety equipment to climb the aerial ladder. All of these actions, when done after a lot of practice, are very quick and smooth.

The victim was approximately 60 feet off the ground in the window. There were no obstructions like electric wires and tree limbs. Therefore, making it an easy reach for Ladder 1 once it got up and being raised. It was simply a race against time at this point. Could the Ladder 1 be raised to the college male before he could take no more smoke and heat and jump from that window? The answer to the question came quickly.

One could only imagine what the fire conditions were like in the attic at the moment of decision time. The fire had begun in the basement and traveled through the interior walls until fire and smoke filled the attic with intense black, suffocating smoke. At this time, the fire victim made his desperate decision. As other firefighter units arrived, the aerial was being raised, and firefighters were advancing water on the fire. The young man left the window and crawled out onto a small ledge surrounding the building. Regardless of pleadings by firefighters to be patient, he jumped.

As he let go of the building, I assumed his clear intent was to drop from the 60-foot height, feet first. However, for reasons unknown, something caught his pants as he let go to fall. Whether it was a gutter, roof element, or possibly one of the small roof deicing devices, his body was immediately spun headfirst during his desperate attempt to escape the burning attic. Alcohol consumption may have also been a significant factor affecting his fall. Unfortunately......

While the young man probably had every thought of landing on grass below, as a result of his jump, he was now falling headfirst. Unfortunately, at the bottom of the building, directly under him, was a concrete enclosure for a staircase allowing deliveries into the basement. In summary, as a result of the jump, he fell headfirst when his only chance of slim survival would have been feet first. As we reached him, it was clear that he had died. The young man had hit the concrete enclosure headfirst. The fall had killed him instantly.

The victim's skull was crushed, and God only knows how many other broken bones he sustained. Given the exposed brain matter in his ears and an obviously broken neck, our decision to declare him deceased was sadly made in the enclosure he landed in. Steve and I bundled him up in one of our yellow disposable blankets and placed him in the having just-arrived Medic Unit 3 for conveyance to a local hospital. It's frustrating to think we needed just 2 more minutes to get to him. Just 2 more fucking minutes to keep him from crossing the fine red line between life and death. If the "fine red line" confuses you, just ask any volunteer or career firefighter about it. They see it crossed too many times in their years of service.

One can only imagine the fire conditions in the attic that would force an individual to look at a 60-foot freefall and make the conscious decision to jump. Firefighters were so close to getting to him. We could see him, and he could see us coming for him. Had those cars not been illegally parked and blocking the way of travel for fire companies, firefighters would have saved him.

It was discovered after the fire there was an additional private party space in the attic where he was first spotted. The senior members of the fraternity and its officers had exclusive rights to the rooms on the top floor. Over time, the students had cut holes in their bedroom ceilings, allowing the senior members to use a small ladder to climb up into the attic area, which was off-limits to other frat members. The attic space had been made into a private party area with a bar, games, couches, and over-stuffed chairs.

These man-made openings into the attic also created a natural chimney effect throughout the building for the fire that quickly drew flames, heat, and smoke into the attic area from the basement, mainly, given the building's balloon construction. Firefighters easily understand the travel of fire and smoke through an older building like this. Hidden fire in the walls was quickly drawn to the attic, just as fire would be by a chimney, and created the horrific conditions that would cause the young man to consider jumping from the window.

Losing a victim in fire is personalized by firefighters as a failure of the very core mission of every firefighter. When firefighters first arrive at active fires, excitement is high. There are a lot of tasks to perform, people to protect, and equipment to manage. Then, after the fire, you'll see hugs and high-fives by volunteer and career firefighters for successfully protecting lives and property.

When a fire victim is lost, a sudden veil of quiet sadness envelops the fire ground. Every firefighter in the fire response feels the failure of this protective primary mission. However, this fire ground loss goes further than just the fire ground. Firefighters from neighboring fire departments will likely feel the loss and extend condolences and words of support to those firefighters who responded to a fire where a fire victim's death occurs. But it often goes even further than that. Firefighters nationwide, who had tragic fires of their own, will understand and sympathize with the firefighters and their recent loss. And as a community service committed to protecting life and property, the fire service will review many of those events surrounding the death and grasp any and all lessons that may lead to learning how to prevent life loss in the future. Fire deaths have a very significant impact on the fire service.

While the reasons surrounding this university fire death can be studied, understood, and explained, it doesn't erase the fact that a healthy college-aged young man lost his life in this fire. Yet, except for the illegally parked cars that night, this young man might very well be alive. For indeed, too much time was wasted getting around that alley corner. Our response was delayed without a doubt.

Firefighters searched throughout the building that night for other victims possibly trapped or in need of rescue. A first (primary) search was conducted by Ladder 6, followed by a secondary search of all four floors. The floors below the attic were relatively clear of smoke and heat, and the visibility was good. Unfortunately, this fire had traveled vertically through the walls, so our overhaul of the fire building and looking for hidden fire, would require labor intensive effort opening the walls and putting out spot fires. Unfortunately, this fire had raced so quickly from the basements to the attic caused by those room openings through the fourth-floor ceilings.

Investigators quickly determined the cause of the fire. A homeless individual had taken refuge for the cold night in the sub-basement area of the frat and had fallen asleep smoking. It was assumed with all the partying, people coming and going, and the additional alcohol consumption, this homeless person had gone undetected by frat members. Unfortunately, the intruder's bedding ignited, and rather than warn partygoers about the fire he had accidentally started, he simply ran from the building, allowing the fire to continue to burn and grow.

The frat was considered a balloon-constructed building. Balloon frame construction consists of a wooden structure and lumber elements holding the structure together. Firefighters are familiar with balloon frames as they were among the first wooden construction methods used in older buildings. A lightweight timber frame would be constructed around the columns that run continuously from the bottom of the building to the top floor of the building. The roof would typically be a truss structure consisting of slopping rafters and ceiling joists. We, as firefighters, are very familiar with this type of construction. This explains why when firefighters are called to a basement fire in a balloon-constructed building, similar to fighting a fire in a bank vault, it's common to see suddenly fire appear in the attic and eaves and no fire in the floors in between except the fire contained in the walls.

That night, city police took the opportunity to put $500 tickets on each of the thirty cars blocking any hope of getting to the victim. The tickets were issued prior to the cars being towed away at the owners' expense.

I've never really known why people think there's tension between police officers and firefighters. In my personal experience, firefighters, paramedics, and law enforcement personnel were close, very close, on the streets. I guess it makes for good television if there's a friction between fire and police departments. Honestly, we needed the police to protect us. They needed us to take care of them quickly during a traumatic injury of an officer. And both police and firefighters knew it was far easier to clean an ambulance of vomit, blood, poop, and pee than to clean the back seat of a police squad car. Working into all hours of the night meant working closely with law enforcement with the greatest respect and admiration. Besides, there were also a large number of after-midnight emergency room cups of coffee sharing stories among police and firefighters.

Fire lanes exist for a reason. Due to the size of fire trucks, firefighters need the space to get in and out of tight roadways. Please avoid blocking them. And this might have been a completely different outcome had there been sprinklers in this structure. Sprinkler systems have been done a great dis-service by Hollywood productions. They don't flood buildings. They put out or control fires until firefighters arrive. Simple as that.

Always have and practice what firefighters call, a Home Escape Plan. Simply stated, two safe ways out of each room in the house.

"Firefighters are the ones who make a difference in the world, one person at a time."

—Anonymous

CHAPTER 8

RING CUTTER HEROS

It doesn't take much for a fire station crew to hang a nickname on a firefighter. Our department had nicknames like The Arm, Bull, Brownie, Fast Eddie, Dozer, Bags, Winky, etc. My nickname was Ski. Firefighters recognize nicknames as a respectful and traditional part of fire service and the fire service culture. The nicknames can derive from many different sources within the fire service. Sometimes, acts of bravery, repeated behaviors, unusual hobbies, and, more commonly, a twist on a firefighter's name. But the scariest source is a nickname's foundation based on a strange call or, in the case below, emergency responses.

Sometimes, a nickname is earned when fighting a fire, like a successful automobile extrication or breaching a super challenging wall, door, or window. A nickname may come from a firefighter cutting a roof opening on the top of a burning building. Maybe a nickname is earned by quickly climbing a ladder to reach the fire victim. Those nicknames are earned daily across the fire service of the United States, and those amazing firefighting actions are constantly earning the fire service reputations and nicknames. However, again one worries about nicknames earned during not-so-positive acts or strange emergencies.

"Attention Medic 1, 804 Franklin Street, Apartment 4, for a medical emergency. Time out 8:58 pm."

Steve and I stopped our basketball game with the other firefighters of Station One and ran to Medic Unit One. While en route to Franklin Street, the 911 dispatcher provided further information indicating our patient was a young man in severe abdominal pain. Initial dispatches to the station were usually just for the units requested. Once the units were en route, the dispatchers would pass along any additional information they had gotten from the caller. Dispatch didn't provide much information for this Franklin Street request for paramedics, just "severe abdominal pain, and the patient was a young male."

Once on location and before we could reach Apartment 4, Steve and I could hear the young male screaming in obvious pain from the hallway above us. Upon entering the patient's apartment, Steve and I discovered a young male about 21 years old. He was most certainly in pain. Our patient was sitting in a chair wearing only a university sweatshirt, but strangely only a towel covered his waist. When Steve removed the towel, we could both immediately see the cause of the patient's abdominal pain. The patient's penis was engorged, misshaped, and oddly discolored. When asked about his dilemma, he informed us he had put a cock ring on for sex earlier in the day and tried unsuccessfully to remove it for the past several hours.

Steve and I couldn't remember specific cock ring training in our paramedic schooling, and, to be honest, neither of us had ever heard of a cock ring. We were informed by the patient these cock rings are sexual enhancement devices. Wearing the ring allowed blood to flow into the penis while restricting the return of blood, resulting in bigger and longer-lasting erections.

Our patient had tried everything to remove the ring throughout the early evening hours. We could certainly understand his pain and his desperate desire to remove it. Steve and I decided, however, rather than waste time messing around with the patient's erection and his dilemma, we opted for immediate conveyance to a local hospital.

Our department paramedics, by policy, always called ahead to emergency rooms to let the hospital staff know we were on our way to them and provide a patient update. I think this was the shortest report to any emergency room Steve ever gave.

Over years of working together, all career and volunteer paramedics and EMTs develop excellent relationships with their emergency room staff. Countless cups of coffee are shared over calls, and patient updates with the docs and nurses make for a very close team when chaotic and challenging calls occur. Steve's radio report was the most gentle and respectful radio transmission he could have provided. It was the first and only time I ever heard him avoid discussing someone's situation in such delicate and medical terms.

Understandably, our patient was very uncomfortable and constantly asked if he would possibly lose his penis in this ordeal. The question of amputation was clearly in our patient's thoughts. We assured him repeatedly that he would be okay and that once the cock ring was removed, things should return to normal. We were unsure of the last part of that sentence, but the medical professionals would assess any damage and give him the truth once we arrived at the emergency room. It's safe to say we were also laughing under our breath and outward concern.

Once at the emergency room, our patient with his erection was loaded onto the exam room bed. We left the exam room to write the report and clean the ambulance in order to place our medic unit back in service and be ready for our next call. We were both interested to see if there was a code for penis in our medical computer database. There wasn't. We wondered what the fire department's administrative staff reviewing reports would think when they saw the "cock ring" report early the following week. We had no idea about these sexual enhancement devices, but now we do. Oh well, it was what it was, and Steve and I were always willing to learn.

It wasn't long before we were approached by one of the emergency room nurses asking if we possibly had a ring cutter on our Medic 1. We did. I had never thought about the ring cutter before now, but we certainly had one. All city Medic Units carried them.

One might be surprised by how often ring cutters are needed and used. They are really slick tools to use. Whether children, teenagers, grown or senior adults, there come times when a ring becomes too small or some swelling has occurred to make the rings uncomfortable. Some rings come off after time, and some don't. A ring cutter makes the job of ring removal easy.

The only way to describe a ring cutter is to think of a pair of needle nose pliers. Only on a ring cutter, on one of the noses (or jaws), rests a circular diamond blade about the size of a dime. Attached to this small diamond saw is a small handle allowing one to turn the blade like a circular saw. The other needle nose jaw without the cutter is slid carefully under the ring. The needle nose jaw with the cutter is brought down to meet the ring's metal, and one starts turning the small saw handle. Slowly the metal is cut, and once cut, the ends of the ring can be pulled apart, separated, and the ring removed.

The ring cutter is a commonly used tool for paramedics and EMTs. In the past, our paramedics once used a ring cutter to remove an entire doorknob from a child's finger. It took about two hours and five blades (not cheap) to remove the doorknob from the finger of a 3-year-old. A family had walked into their station with their minor child's finger caught through the lock of an ordinary doorknob. According to the father, the child put his finger in the doorknob lock in their garage while playing with some hardware lying around his workbench. But, back to our patient's penis.

After we retrieved the ring cutter from our medic unit and gave it to the ER staff, Steve and I returned to writing our emergency response report. It was only a matter of minutes before the emergency room doctor joined us and asked if we would be so kind as to cut the ring off our young patient's penis. They were having trouble using ours.

Sure thing. We'll try. The emergency room staff had tried lubricants without success, so emergency room staff thought we firefighters might be better able to help. Like we knew just what to do. This entire medic response had already been educational, funny, strange, and outside our training. So what else did they want us to do? The universe was getting back at us for laughing so much in the report room. Karma sucks.

After gloving up with surgical gloves, Steve and I entered the exam room. We certainly got the patient's attention when he saw the piece of equipment Steve was holding onto. The lube made it really easy to slide the ring cutter into position. So, as one of us (not saying who) stabilized the young man's penis with a gloved hand, the other paramedic (not saying who) started to cut away the ring safely. Once we cut through the metal, we pulled the two metal ends of the rings apart with another standard pair of needle nose pliers. Not surprisingly, the patient felt immediate relief. With the ring removed, there was no longer a need for the patient's worry about amputation. Once the ring was removed, everything would or should return to normal according to the medical staff.

It's unfortunate this emergency room was such a busy place. While performing our miracles of medical removal of the ring, other department medic units were arriving with their patients. They heard about what we were doing from the emergency room staff. After the expected ribbing from colleagues, we loaded up our medic unit to return to Station One. All the while knowing this story would go through the fire department stations like wildfire. Finally, we returned to Station One to finish the rest of our work shift.

Our crew left at 7 am the following day, but not without comments in the kitchen during early morning coffee about the now infamous cock ring call the night before. We only had 24 hours off between shifts. Our department firefighters worked a 48-hour schedule. We would be on duty during the week, 24 hours on Monday, Wednesday, and Friday. After Friday's shift, we would be off 4 days before returning to the station. When spread out over the month and year and with extra shifts off, it all added up to 48 hours a week.

Following our 24 hours off, we returned to start our new shift at 7 am Wednesday morning. Morning coffee was lively that Wednesday. Our previous day's run invited laughter, unbelievable teasing, and a lot of ribbing. Someone was even kind enough to share with us how quickly our adventures in the emergency room on Monday had spread through the department. Complete with the recommendation that cock ring training should be now required of all paramedics.

That Wednesday was an uneventful day. There were several medical calls, but only one was significantly bad and noteworthy. A young woman was discovered by her neighbors around 3:15 pm, unconscious on her front lawn. Both the police and fire departments responded. The young woman had just left her home and was going to pick up her young son at a local elementary school.

As Medic 1 arrived at the location, she was lying in the grass with several police officers trying to investigate exactly what had happened. Was she hit? Was this a medical emergency? Did she fall? Police had not yet determined exactly what happened to cause this young woman to be unconscious lying in the yard. As Steve and I got to the patient's side, we found her with a rapid faint pulse, unreadable blood pressure, and very slow and shallow breathing.

It was very confusing because no one around could explain what happened to cause this woman to collapse, and the patient couldn't help either. When we opened her shirt to begin an examination of her heart with our EKG and to listen to her breathing sounds, we found a small spot of blood on her bra. The blood was just under her left breast. When we lifted the bra to see the possible cause, a small trickle of blood ran down her chest and along her side. It was coming from a wound no larger than the diameter of an aspirin. No doubt about the cause now. She had been stabbed.

Given the cause being a likely stabbing to her chest and not knowing the size of the knife or stabbing instrument, the patient was a "load and go." Steve and I would waste no more time with our examination. "Stop whatever you're doing, load to the stretcher, and GO! We tried an IV of lactate ringers on our way to Trauma Center, but without success because her veins collapsed due to blood loss internally. If she were to live, she needed a chest surgeon right now and the expertise of the emergency room staff.

Our patient was declared dead before we could finish our reports—another fine line between life and death crossed by a very young mother. During our attempts to intubate the patient, Steve had used a stylet. A stylet is a long narrow bendable metal rod that paramedics use to guide the endotracheal tube into the trachea. Detectives would soon arrive at Station One to ensure the tool was ours and not possibly a murder weapon. It was ours. Steve had dropped it on the lawn when we decided to quickly transport our patient.

At 10 pm that day, we again found ourselves in the emergency report room. Steve and I were there for a simple conveyance of an elderly male with belly pain. While working on the report, the emergency room staff approached us again with a request. It seems they had another young male patient in one of the exam rooms with a cock ring and again unable to be removed with lubricant. Seeing our unit, the emergency room charge nurse sheepishly asked if we would be so kind as to once again remove another cock ring. We asked again why they hadn't been able to secure a ring cutter for their emergency room, and they told us they were still awaiting the delivery of one.

We agreed to once again remove another young man's cock ring. While my partner gloved up to stabilize the patient's penis, I started the cutting process again and reestablished the patient's blood flow. Not surprisingly, other arriving medic units were aware of our assistance and medical feats again in the emergency room. Word spread again quickly, and we once again finished our 24-hour shift. Two 24-hour work shifts back-to-back, and two cock rings.

Another 24 hours off, only to return on Friday morning at 7 am. This would be the last shift day before having the next 4 days off. Holy crap, the Friday morning coffee was even more robust than before, with comments and jokes shared regarding another shift that had passed and another cock ring removed. One of the officers suggested that Steve and I open a cock ring removal business. Sell them and then remove them. Ha ha. All we could do was read the newspapers, drink coffee, and remain unaffected by the steady flow of comments coming our way. The department's

Assistant Chief even stopped into Station One for coffee with the crew and had something snarky to say regarding our cock ring experiences during two 24-hour work shifts in a row.

It would be a typical Friday. Busy with numerous medic and fire calls in a preweekend busy city. The medic calls were normal, if there's such a thing, throughout the day. Some were medical in nature. Some traumatic, like bike falls and minor car accidents. My partner Steve and I, at one point, responded to a fight in a local café. Police had arrived, and all we had to do was evaluate the combatants. The best we could tell the fight was a disagreement over the last piece of the pie on a plate. Typical Friday, I guess.

Station One firefighters had a small "room and contents" fire in the student dorms. An over-cooked bag of popcorn had caught fire in the microwave, and while the smoke stunk like hell, Engine 1 could extinguish it while Ladder 1 and Medic 1 ventilated the building of stinky smoke. Then, after a couple of calls for kids drinking too much in the university area bars, we were able to get to the bunks for sleep around 1:30 am.

At around 4 am, the lights in our paramedic bedroom suddenly came on. Hearing our names, strangely, we weren't awoken by the station alarm going off. Instead, in the doorway stood our Captain. He asked us to get up and informed us we were requested to go to the emergency room of one of the city's hospitals. They needed a medic unit and ring cutter. As Medic 1 was the closest unit to the hospital, Steve and I were sent.

We laughed and kidded each other as to why we were sent. No, it couldn't be. All we knew at that time in the morning was the emergency room staff needed a ring cutter. When we arrived, the emergency room staff told us why the request came at such an early hour. You could have knocked either of us over with a feather. Sure enough, another cock ring is unable to be removed with lubrication.

When asked, the emergency room staff explained they had received their ring cutter but had not enough blade wheels for the metal cutting. Another 15 minutes later, the ring was off. Steve and I were getting faster at this, or was it just my imagination? Another cock ring was removed. Three consecutive shifts and three separate, random, and unrelated cock ring removals. Never saw another one, ever, after these three. As for our reputations and nicknames… never changed. Lucky us.

Time passed; I estimate 15 years. I had gone onto work for the United States Fire Administration in Washington DC, and I had the opportunity to revisit my home city. Many of my Station One colleagues had long retired from the city fire department. While walking around the Station One apparatus floor with a friend with so many memories of days gone by, a former firefighter I recognized appeared. It seems this once young Station One rookie on our shift had grown up to become a shift Battalion Chief and immediately recognized and remembered me. He called a couple of other young firefighters on shift that day down for some introductions.

After some friendly greetings, handshakes, and discussion, my friend asked the Battalion Chief what memory he had of my time in the fire department. Forget the hundreds of fires, the countless number of medical emergencies, babies delivered, and the countless number of fire inspections and just helping residents and business owners of the community.

The Chief immediately went to my cock ring removal stories from many years before. I was with FEMA at this time, in service to the United States Fire Administrator, and this is the image given to these young firefighters. The summation of my career. Oh well, my reputation and fond memories of Steve were made even more poignant now that Steve has left this planet due to cancer. I cannot wait to share with him the fire department reputation we earned together. I'm sure we'll be laughing together again someday.

For sure, we can laugh at the unbelievable predicaments the three young men found themselves in. But the next time you see a fire truck or ambulance with lights and sirens moving through the streets of your community, you'll feel secure knowing they go when individuals call for firefighters. And when firefighters go, firefighters respond with solutions and dedication to your safety. Regardless of the needs of the callers.

Someone on the other end of an emergency response has asked for firefighters because they have found themselves in unmanageable chaotic situations. Community members need the solutions and assistance these dedicated volunteer and career firefighters offer. No one ever calls 911 on their best days. Firefighters are always invited into the 911 caller's worse day.

Volunteer and career firefighters are just "doing for others."

"Firefighters are the ones who see the worst of humanity and still believe in the best."

— Anonymous

CHAPTER 9

HERE ONE MOMENT.... GONE THE NEXT

Some of the most challenging calls firefighters respond to are vehicle accidents. They're difficult for many reasons. First, with the wide variety of vehicles on the roadways, from small to large, electric, diesel or gasoline, passenger cars to trucks with freight, or on its side or roof, firefighters only know a little about the vehicles or accidents until they arrive on location.

The speed involved in the accident relates to the extent of damage encountered by first responders. Additionally, the motor vehicle accident environment requires firefighters, EMS, and police personnel to work on roadways where cars passing by move fast, and there may also be reduced visibility. Unfortunately, a number of firefighters and EMTs lose their lives on the Nation's highways as a result of drunk drivers. In days gone by, it was all too common for emergency vehicles to park in such a way as to minimize road blockage of lanes of travel. As far to the right as possible. Nowadays it's common to see large fire trucks blocking as many lanes as are needed to block in order to protect all first responders on the scene.

The list of hazards faced by responders on roadways is long. Far too many firefighters, EMS personnel, and law enforcement officers have been critically injured and given a lifetime of rehabilitation or, unfortunately, lost their lives working on America's highways.

Motor vehicle accidents become more tragic and complex, especially among volunteer firefighters in smaller communities when the responders likely know the victims. There have been numerous stories of volunteer firefighters extricating their own children from tragic vehicle accidents.

Recently, in one small community in Pennsylvania, an automobile collided with a truck head-on after crossing a center line around 3:30 pm one afternoon. As a result of the accident, five young teenagers were killed instantly, having just left their local high school. No alcohol or drugs were involved. The volunteer department that responded knew all five of the children on the scene, all dead, but their bodies were still trapped in their vehicle needing to be extricated. One can only imagine the healing and mental scarring one call in the late afternoon would have on these firefighters in months and years ahead. Motor vehicle accidents are terrible.

Station 5 was a wonderful station to be detailed to for a 24-hour shift. High volumes of heart and difficulty breathing-related calls were more the norm for Medic Unit 5. Every call required long patient conveyances of up to an hour or more to go to any one of the city's four emergency rooms and return to the fire station. The Station 5 first-run territory grew quickly with the city boundaries expanding rapidly, with an ever-growing number of newer homes, new businesses, and a significant senior population. The result was lower fire response demands due to the newer building construction but higher medic unit requests due to population diversity. There were also a lot of new small entrepreneurial manufacturing facilities. Looking at the service demands of Station 5, it could be of no wonder this station was referred to as the "retirement station." But it was an excellent daily escape from the daily grind of downtown stations and my Station One.

The morning coffee was alive with the typical station banter. Had a public citizen walked into the kitchen from the outside, the firefighter conversations would have made little sense. As I was usually assigned to downtown Station One, and it was enjoyable to hear so many different opinions on today's personal news. It was common for little competitions to surface throughout the day to make things in the stations interesting. These challenges added a little bit to each day.

At this morning's coffee, Ed, the Engine 5 driver, commented that he had discovered boiling water would freeze faster than an ordinary glass of tap water when placed in a freezer. This topic was of immediate interest to the entire station crew. Bets were made to back up Ed's hypothesis. Then, of course, there was the expected pushback and calls of "bullshit" to this firefighter-turned-scientist and his frozen water claims.

The topics of the day over coffee included the ever-changing economy. There were American hostages in a foreign country needing our solutions, and the fishing season was about to open. All were topics worthy of continual firefighter conversations. Still, the station personnel remained focused on the freezing water statement made by Eddy. The discussions throughout the station, during morning chores and general cleaning, led to the ever-growing possibility of an ice cream bet, a very big event in station life indeed: ice cream for the crew, including all the toppings.

The bet became official as the crew assembled for the mid-morning coffee and peanut butter toast around 9:15 am. Eddy maintained his undisputable scientific position that boiling water freezes before an equal amount of tap temperature water. Engine 5 driver, Harold, an old-timer and Ladder 5 driver, finally challenged the concept. Ed's theory was finally challenged officially by another firefighter willing to risk the money on ice cream for the crew. And Harold's picture is in the dictionary for the definition of "tight wad."

Immediately, the firefighters of Station 5 identified and agreed upon the two identical containers for the challenge. They filled one plastic glass with room-temperature water from the kitchen tap. In another identical plastic glass was the same amount of boiling water. The crew confirmed both as even and placed them in the station freezer. And so the test began. The rules were simple enough. No one could open the freezer without everyone being present. To further ensure the security of the freezer, the cook, Dennis, was assigned as the freezer's royal guard. If you couldn't trust Dennis, the cook, whom could you trust? The Engine 5 Captain would serve as the final judge.

Just before lunch, it was time to check the status of the water experiment. Several crew members, including the two combatants, gathered at the freezer for the first check. They opened the freezer slowly and, to the surprise of everyone, made a strange discovery. The regular tap water glass showed signs of freezing. But on the other hand, the container with the boiling water was still hot and showed no signs of getting cold. Nevertheless, the combatants, especially Eddy, held firmly to their beliefs. Even though it was still hot, the glass with the boiling water would freeze faster than the tap water container. Just be patient.

The Captain and Ed decided to check the freezer every 30 minutes to ensure the crew would witness when freezing was accomplished. Following the 11:30 pm lunch, the Captain decided that a final check would occur soon. We were losing inspection and training time with this experiment, and the Captain was no doubt anxious to get going on his afternoon activities before a Battalion Chief showed up.

The final unveiling was to take place at 12:30 pm. When the time arrived to open the freezer and pull out the glasses, the experiment would end, and the loser would buy ice cream. The container with tap water was frozen solid in many places. Surprisingly, the container with the boiling water was still hot to the touch. The boiling water container remained the same. Eddie owed the crew ice cream with the toppings of their choice.

Before continuing, as Mr. Paul Harvey would have said, "And now for the rest of the story." Dennis, the station's most honest cook ever, and Eddy's good friend, was slyly smiling. Working in the kitchen while all the other Station 5 firefighters were out drilling and cleaning, Dennis wasn't just taking care of his usual routine of cooking meals for the day. Dennis apparently would reach into the freezer every half hour or so and replace the boiling water container with fresh boiling water. There was no way that firefighter Eddy was going to win. The truth never came out; however, a couple of us were in on the scam. Afterall, someone had to keep Eddy out of the kitchen. The ice cream with all the toppings was wonderful that day, thanks to Eddy, or maybe we should thank Dennis. Eddy could afford to lose. The rest of the day was uneventful, except for a few medical calls.

"Attention Medic 5, Ladder 5, Medic 3, Squad 1, and BC, along with Engine 5, report of an accident with entrapment at the intersection of State Highway 15 and Kohler Mill Road. Time out midnight."

Accidents were also common in Station 5's territory because of its proximity to the city's boundary edge. A number of major thoroughfares and highways came together and merged in 5's first-run territory. Several of the roads were notoriously high-speed roadways. The intersection we were responding to had long been a problem as it was one of the few places with a stoplight on a high-speed stretch of road. However, the city's traffic patterns had outgrown the usefulness of these highway stoplights. Major reconstruction projects were in the plans for the city, but those plans meant nothing on this night.

Engine 5 was already out on the streets from an earlier call. Engine 5 crew was returning from a small dumpster fire and was already en route to the accident scene. As my partner Hugh and I boarded Medic 5, still in quarters, and by radio, we were aware Engine 5 had already arrived at the accident location. Engine 5 Captain confirmed the accident and the entrapment of the female driver.

Given the severity of the accident by Engine 5 and the turns and double clutching to operate Ladder 5, the Ladder 5 officer waved for Medic 5 not to wait for them and get going. As we pulled out into the cool night, our red lights seemed to bounce off structures everywhere. Particularly noticeable were our lights flashing off the concrete overpass we were merging onto. Once on state Highway 15, it was only a mile or so to the intersection and accident scene. Once we merged onto the highway, we could see the emergency lights of many emergency vehicles in the distance. This view was all surreal to me, having just gotten pulled out of a sound sleep and still trying to clear my thoughts.

When Hugh pulled us into the accident scene, Engine 5 was busy stabilizing the crushed vehicle. One could easily imagine accident responses in years gone by with firefighters using hack saws, circular saws, and sledge hammers to open the metal of a crushed vehicle. Instead, our department's approach to vehicle accidents was stabilizing the vehicles. Given the possibility of further head and neck injuries from tearing an unstable vehicle apart, causing fires from fuels and the sparks of saws, and causing even greater injuries to patients, stabilizing the vehicle and scene was the first priority. This procedure reduced the risk of injuries to firefighters and paramedics as well. Stabilize the vehicles and get paramedics inside the crash vehicle to evaluate patients. Accidents were no longer just a process of pulling people out willy-nilly without regard to further injuries and even death.

Engine 5 had made room for Medic 5 to be located close to the vehicles involved. It was apparent this was a T-Bone accident. The worse kind of accident of all. Cars were designed for safety at that time should you be struck in the front or the rear, but not from the side. T-Bone accidents were side hits, offering no protection to vehicle occupants. As was the case with this accident. The first and foremost goals are to get paramedics to the patients. Assess the patient's vitals and potential injury status and work with firefighters outside the vehicle to determine the most expedient and safest extrication method for the patient.

The damage to the vehicle and the drunk driver that T-Boned this vehicle, causing the accident, was minimal. The driver causing the accident had a cut to the bridge of his nose and was inebriated. However, the damage to the car that was T-Boned was very significant. Imagine, if you will, a vehicle being struck on the side by another bigger vehicle going more than 60 miles per hour, as estimated by police on the scene of our accident. The driver's side door is now where the center counsel once was. The mangled steering wheel acted like a vice trapping arms and limbs under it. Glass was everywhere, including in the cuts and lacerations of victims. A dashboard was now crushing the occupant amid torn shreds of plastic, metal, and instrumentation wiring and components. The engine compartment was now visible through the car's firewall.

Using the jaws of life to lift the crushed dashboard, Engine 5 and Ladder 5 could gain access to the female we had been told about under the crushed dashboard. Unfortunately, she had ended up under the dash and up against the firewall and engine of the vehicle. She was almost totally out of sight from her belly button to the top of her head, with only her waist and legs showing obvious fractures. She wore a beautiful dress, although covered with blood, and was undoubtedly dead on arrival. (DOA).

The impact of the accident had snapped her neck hard enough to expose her spinal cord, which had been unseen until the dashboard was removed and a flashlight was available. The young lady was wearing the formal dress because she had been coming from a local high school prom and was dressed for the evening. There was nothing humanly possible we could do for her. No question she was DOA. We could slow down our efforts at this point.

Her removal from the vehicle required the removal of the passenger side door. Truck 5 made quick work of this door removal with the Jaws of Life. Unfortunately, an arm fell out of the new door opening when it was removed. Holy shit, there was another person in the car. Back to work for Hugh and me, and another adrenaline dump for all firefighters on the scene.

Although it could probably be explained, there's no way to understand how the driver ended up under the deceased female in this accident. A quick check showed a very faint carotid pulse and a very unconscious young man. The female was quickly removed and set temporarily on the roadway, covered in one of our yellow disposable blankets. It was very obvious this young man was bleeding internally with several chest fractures.

A decision needed to be made rapidly by Hugh and me. We were worried about attending to the compound femur fracture, multiple cuts, and lacerations or dealing with the patient's impending death due to having no blood volume. Our patient needed to be extricated immediately and conveyed to an emergency room and awaiting surgeons. We decided to remove the young man as quickly as possible and make a rapid conveyance to an emergency room. We would start large IVs while en route to the hospital. Engine 5 firefighters brought our stretcher from Medic 5 to the car with MAST pants already laid out for the patient to be placed in.

Medical Anti-Shock Trousers (MAST), also known as military anti-shock trousers or pneumatic anti-shock garments (PASG), are medical devices made of synthetic inflatable air bladders which are applied to a patient's abdomen, pelvis, and lower extremities. These devices include one abdominal compartment and two leg compartments that attach to a pump with valves to control the pressure within the air bladders. The concept of these devices is simple; apply pressure to the lower extremities and abdomen to shift or push the patient's own blood volume from the abdomen, pelvis, and lower extremities to the upper body and central brain, heart, and lung circulation.

Our patient was quickly loaded onto the stretcher, into the MAST pants, and moved into Medic 5. An extra firefighter from Engine 5 was provided to drive Hugh and me to the emergency room, allowing both of us to work in the back of Medic 5. Our destination was the Trauma One Emergency Room. We were racing against time to get this young man to a surgical team.

Once on board Medic 5 and en route to the Emergency Room, our patient was given large volumes of Lactated Ringers, the closest fluid we had on board Medic 5 to fight against blood loss. Ringer's lactate is a mixture of sodium chloride, sodium lactate, potassium chloride, and calcium chloride in water. It replaces fluids and electrolytes in patients with low blood volume or blood pressure. However, no matter how much we pumped into his veins, we clearly needed more fluid. A quick discussion with the Department's Medical Director resulted in permission for Hugh and me to inflate the MAST pants.

These MAST pants were relatively new to the department. We had been trained in their use and told of the incredible results when applied to patients who were bleeding to death. So, with the go-ahead we received from our Medical Doctor, Hugh and I inflated the pants. To our astonishment, as soon as the pants started to inflate that night, the patient began to awaken from his unconscious state. During MAST training, we had heard several amazing results from the MAST inflations, but witnessing firsthand the impact on our patient was a miracle. This young man was suddenly waking, asking questions, and talking clearly with us.

Sadly, one of his first questions was about his girlfriend's condition. We lied. We didn't want to tell him she was a motor vehicle fatality statistic and under a yellow blanket at the accident scene. She was in the hands of other paramedics and coroner, and while it looked bad, we had no way of contacting the other Medic Unit. We lied, but we didn't care at that point. He had several other questions, like what happened, was anyone else hurt, how was his dad's car, and so on.

There are many events volunteer and career first responders of Fire, EMS, and Law Enforcement witness every day, but do we understand some of the things that are said and done in life-and-death situations? Hugh and I suspected our patient had some idea of just how badly he was hurt when he turned to us and made us promise we would tell his mom he "loved her." Holy shit. How does one respond to a request like that? At the time, all one can say is yes to the promise but reassure the patient he will be okay and not to worry because he will be able to tell his mom himself.

Many last words are spoken in the back of Medic Units across the United States daily. For the most part, these last messages are statements of love. Mom, Dad, siblings, wife, and children are the prominent recipients of these last moment of life statements. Sometimes, these remaining last words are about forgiveness. They are forgiving someone for something or asking for forgiveness. So sad. And a very heavy burden to bear for career and volunteers working on ambulances.

While en route to the Level One Trauma emergency room, there was a change in our patient's desire to be taken to another hospital emergency room. The patient, now awake and oriented to time and place, insisted on being taken to his hospital of choice. To the hospital his family always used and the hospital he was born in. In this case, with the patient being conscious, he had the right to determine what emergency room he wished to go to. He needed a Level One Trauma Center, we advised him of this, but, in this case, the hospital he chose was an excellent facility with full medical expertise available by phone. And this facility was the closest hospital, saving us an additional 10-15 minutes of travel. We diverted to the hospital of his choice. We called ahead on the radio to ensure the emergency room was aware of the severity of the patient's injuries and to give their medical teams a head start in preparation for our patient.

Once in the emergency room, the patient was transferred to their staff, and their medical teams took over. While Hugh ensured that our Medic Unit was cleaned, resupplied, and put back in service, I retreated to the room the hospital set aside for our run and computer reporting. While sitting at the computer, we heard a sudden call for a hospital-wide call for CODE BLUE medical response to the Emergency Room. The sudden energy rush of medical personnel and equipment was palpable; The activity was centered around the intake exam room where we had just transferred our accident patient.

All of the hallway activities indicated our accident patient had crashed (taken a turn for the worse). At that point, Hugh and I were anxious to get down to the exam room to see what was occurring and offer assistance if needed.

After 20 minutes of frantic activities and the medical staff rushing in many directions to retrieve equipment, order a test, or work on our patient, now their patient, the young man's declaration of death was announced. The young man just talking to us in the Medic Unit 20 minutes ago, was lying lifeless now in the Emergency Room.

As cold as it may sound, it was now a good time to retrieve and clean our MAST pants and return them to service. They were expensive medical tools and our department wished we retrieved them whenever possible. To our astonishment and anger, we quickly realized the MAST pants had been cut open with scissors. Not normally deflated through the valves as usual but cut with medical scissors. Are you fucking kidding me? Who in their right mind would cut open a pair of MAST pants? The deflation valves are right there for everyone to see. And Hugh and I would have been more than happy to control the deflation had we been asked. But we were never asked. The emergency doc on duty had fucked up.

Imagine, if you will, a shot glass full of blood. Ick. But go with me on this. So full and can't accept more, and the shot glass has served its purpose. Now pour the shot glass into an empty gallon container. Barely enough to cover the bottom. Well, that is what happens with the sudden release of the MAST pants. You allow the vital life-sustaining volume of blood used by the heart, lungs, and brain to flow into the abdomen and legs. Blood pressure immediately drops, and the pulse disappears. To a victim of trauma leaking blood somewhere, this sudden release is a death sentence.

Upon follow-up and with the promise of secrecy to the Emergency Room nurses we talked to, we discovered the ER Doctor wanted to tap the patient's belly for blood and got pissed that the MAST pants were in his way. Without any thought or request for guidance from trained personnel in the room, the doc grabbed a pair of scissors and cut the abdominal bladder as he felt. While it might have been highly unlikely, our vehicle accident patient would have survived his injuries, but when the pants were cut, any and all chances were eliminated. The ER doc caused our patient's immediate death.

As pointed out earlier, all firefighters face horrendous challenges in and around accident scenes. Besides the obvious trauma and its long-lasting impact on one's psychological well-being, firefighters join in witnessing together the fine line between being here today and suddenly gone. One second there's a very young couple, full of life and with beautiful dreams and futures ahead, and in a nanosecond, they're both gone. The young lady in this accident could never have known but for a second what happened. The young man would gain some knowledge during the short period he was conscious, but he too was lost.

The Station 5 crew didn't personally know these two kids they removed from a crushed car. There were no personal connections with either of them. One can only imagine the mental impact of those volunteer firefighters working in more rural areas, where there's a high likelihood of knowing their accident victims. One can only imagine the depth of sorrow they go through in knowing the families and loved ones of the deceased personally. Imagine extricating their lifeless bodies from these tangled puzzles of mangled metal and plastic and witnessing the fine line between here and gone.

And where do you take your thoughts full of mixed and too often angry emotions? Do you take them back to the station? Do you take them to your family when the shift is over? And how could your family possibly understand the emotional happenings on a highway and emergency room? What happens when you look at your own children, regardless of age, knowing about the reality and existence of the fine line between life and death? It's not hard to understand the high divorce rate among firefighters or the ever-growing number of firefighter and EMS personnel suicides.

Firefighters and emergency medical services (EMS) personnel, both volunteer and career, are of the highest importance to ensuring public the safety and health of their communities. Unfortunately, too many of these First Responders are at an elevated risk for suicide because of their work environments, their organizational culture, and occupational and personal stress. This stress can be acute (right now) or chronic (day-to-day stress). Occupational stress in first responders can be associated with the increased risk of mental health issues, including hopelessness, anxiety, depression, and post-traumatic stress, as well as suicidal behaviors such as suicidal ideation (thinking about suicide) and attempts.

During routine shifts, volunteer and career first responders may and often do, experience stress due to the uncertainty in each situation. Stress among first responders can be magnified during emergencies, disasters, pandemics, and other crises. Relationship problems have also been linked to a large proportion of suicides. Extreme family-work demands and stress caused by relationship problems are all too often magnified in this volunteer and career group.

By the way, the promise Hugh and I made to the young man in the back of Medic 5 that night was kept. We told his mother his last words. Tough, but we did make a promise.

"Firefighters are the ones who bring hope to a hopeless situation."

—Anonymous

CHAPTER 10

WHEN YOU KNOW THEM

The Station 4 alert tones opened up:

"Attention Engine 2 and Medic 4 in place of Medic 2, 3610 Poplar Drive for labor and maternity problems. Time out 1:20 pm."

Medic Unit 4 was dispatched to a high-value upscale residential neighborhood in the early afternoon. These neighborhoods were rapidly increasing with the community's rapid growth and the city's rating high on a national magazine's *Best Places to Live* list.

The address given to us was on the very west edge of the city. While close to the address in a new city area, the fire department's new Station 2 would arrive quickly. Unfortunately, the patient's residence was a good 8-9-mile trip for my partner Ken and me on Medic 4. Strangely, this area wasn't the typical neighborhood for a reported labor and delivery emergency call.

Our department was becoming much busier with the ever-growing number of requests for Medic Units and fire truck responses. At the time of our dispatch to Poplar Drive,

Medic 2 was busy with another emergency elsewhere in their territory. When this happened, Medic 4 was needed to cover not only our first-run territory but also the first-run territory of Medic 2. Once we were dispatched to an emergency, the other men and women firefighters and paramedics of the city fire department would cover for Medic 4. Like a well-oiled machine, the on-duty crews worked in harmony to ensure the best emergency responses expected by the community.

My partner Ken and I were happy Engine 2 could get on location at the home of Poplar Drive so fast. The address for the emergency was only a couple of city blocks away from Station 2. With a full crew of four firefighters, they would be able to arrive on-site and manage the chaos quickly. Judging by the dispatcher's stressed tone of voice during the emergency dispatch, Ken and I found ourselves anxiously awaiting a patient update from Engine 2, once on the scene,

From Engine 2's initial radio update, Medic 4 wasn't moving fast enough to reach this patient's address. There was a lot of anxiety and stress in the Engine 2 officer's radio communications pleading for Medic 4 to hurry. But it wasn't long before those dreaded words were heard again over the radio for Medic Unit 4 to "step it up." Engine 2 reported a scene where they were seeing a patient with "massive blood loss."

Once we cleared the usual traffic congestion around Station 4, we found ourselves on very wide-open roadways with long 4-lane straight roads. Medic 4 could move quickly for a vehicle with significant weight balance issues for that time of day in the early afternoon. We could pick up some additional speed in these conditions with fewer intersections, fewer traffic lights, and four travel lanes.

Intersections are incredibly dangerous when our Medic unit is moving this quickly. Not too long ago, our city medic units had federal sirens to announce our emergency response. Many, if not most, fire trucks still have these effective warning sirens. Unfortunately, our newer electronic sirens seemed worthless in letting folks know we were approaching intersections and asking permission from drivers on the road to proceed in spite of red traffic lights. Electronic sirens provide a sense of safety when you're in the vehicle. Still, they're not as effective as the older federal units. Many volunteer and career firefighters complain about their effectiveness and at times report over-driving the sirens.

Wasting no time getting to the emergency, Ken pulled Medic 4 onto a beautiful street with large homes, majestic oaks, and maple trees adorning the landscape. Responding to a maternity emergency in this neighborhood and at this time of day seemed really strange. But, as we pulled into the home's circular driveway behind Engine 2, its crew was already inside the home, pleading for Medic 4 to hurry up.

When firefighters and EMTs enter a home, some emergencies and diseases have their own distinctive smells. For example, one might pick up on the fruity smells of diabetes. One can frequently pick up the smell of alcohol. And there's no mistaking the smell of a DOA. In this emergency, as soon as we entered the doorway, you instantly could smell significant blood loss. And to smell blood, a lot of blood must be present as was the case this day.

As mentioned earlier, this was a neighborhood of substantial and expensive homes. The kind of homes paramedics might have been expected or asked by the owner to remove their shoes before entering as if we would. Instead, we entered through the front foyer. We were immediately met by the officer of Engine 2, whose only words were, "We'll get from the ambulance whatever equipment you need." Those weren't the most reassuring first words I've ever heard. The officer of Engine 2 may not have known the problem, but he certainly knew the severity of the bleeding.

As we left the foyer to enter the living room, we could immediately understand the stress and anxiety we had heard on the radio before arriving. The living room was at one time very decorative, I'm sure. Mountain grey colored carpet and all white furniture. Very welcoming for a home as big as this. Today the living room and dining room were covered in blood. Blood was everywhere—blood on the carpets and the walls. Even the crew from Engine 2 were accumulating blood on their uniforms.

Lying on the couch before us was a young woman covered obviously in her own blood. Engine 2 had waited for our arrival before unclothing her. However, they attempted to control the vaginal bleeding as best they could to comfort the patient. The towels they had used were saturated in blood. She was conscious and, between screams and tears, was asking for both help and for her husband, who was on his way but had not yet arrived.

Despite the blood loss, the patient could answer some quick questions from Ken and me. She, indeed, was pregnant and in her second trimester. Up until that day, our patient reported there had been no problems with her pregnancy. According to the patient, her OB-GYN had been pleased to date with her pregnancy.

She indicated that some bleeding had started about an hour earlier with severe cramping. During this her first pregnancy, she indicated she had an expectation of occasional cramping based on what others had told her. She quickly answered our medical questions. Our first relief was that although her pulse was weak and her blood pressure was very low, she was still conscious and could provide Ken and me with some valuable medical information. Vitals weren't great, but not bad for how much blood we were seeing.

The next step was to pull back her clothing to see the real emergency we were dealing with. As her clothing was lifted, two fetuses were found between her legs—twins of unknown sex and no bigger than hamsters. The fetuses were a reddish purple with umbilical cords still attached and STILL MOVING. Yes, that is correct. They were still moving. Our patient had spontaneously aborted her pregnancy. Oh my God, what a tragedy and even more horrific emotional nightmare this must have been for our patient and her yet-to-arrive husband.

There was absolutely no medical equipment in the city's Medic Units small enough to attempt to save the twins. And what would we be saving? As stated before, it was obviously our patient's worse day, and she was depending on firefighters to provide solutions for something never witnessed before by the Engine 2 crew, Ken, and me—one of our worst OMG moments to date.

The only thing we could think of was to pick up these living fetuses, wrap them in clean towels and run high-flow oxygen into the towel. Everyone knew that if umbilical cords were attached to them, this action taken by me would do nothing for them. I did this more for myself and the patient than actually helping anything. So the umbilical cords were left in place. Our patient quickly became what firefighters identified as a "load and go" conveyance. Load the patient in the medic unit as quickly as possible and race to awaiting medical professionals in the emergency room. Compounding our challenges was the ride to the hospital was a good 15-20 minutes away.

There are many tough decisions that volunteer and career EMS personnel make daily on emergency scenes. The toughest is when you have limited personnel and equipment resources; whom do you save? While we could try some things in the Medic Unit on the trip to the Emergency Room, the mother was our number one priority. Save the mother regardless of the other things suffering going on. Sacrifice the babies if necessary and direct all efforts to save the mother. We got a little break at this point, as the vaginal bleeding had seemed to lessen or almost stop on its own.

Our department Medic units were staffed with two very highly trained firefighter paramedics. During this conveyance, both paramedics needed to be with the patient. A driver was requested and received from the Engine 2 crew. We would protect the twin fetuses en route to the emergency room and try stabilizing the patient's blood pressure with an intravenous drip of lactated ringers. Our Medical Director had given us permission to go ahead with an IV. Contact was made with the patient's choice of the emergency room, and we requested pediatrics and OB/GYN doctors be present upon our arrival.

As the patient was being loaded into the ambulance, I heard my name called out by the patient. Could our patient have known my name from my uniform name tag? Could she have heard my name called out by the Engine 2 crew when we arrived or during the exam and loading onto our stretcher? No, not even close. The patient's name was Susan, and we had graduated from high school in the same class. Unfortunately, as is often the case, we lose touch with our fellow graduates as life happens.

It had been some years since graduation, but this was Susan. The same Susan I sat behind in English and Chemistry classes in high school. Susan was now depending on me to know how to rescue her and save her babies from this chaotic and tragic event. In addition, Susan was expecting me to be honest about the twins. All I could do was assure Susan everything that could be done was being done. The physicians would know more shortly when we arrived at the Emergency Room.

We arrived at the hospital after what seemed like an endless ambulance ride. Susan was offloaded from the ambulance with the twins still wrapped in towels between her legs. Awaiting her arrival was a highly trained team of pediatric professionals and emergency room medical professionals. They immediately went to work on the three patients we brought to them.

When we arrived at the ER, it was the first time we realized just how much blood we had gotten into. My partner and I were covered with blood. Hands and clothing covered. So much blood the Emergency Room staff would let us get out of our uniforms and change into hospital scrub gowns.

We would shower upon return to Station 4. Thanks to the janitorial supplies in the ER, the ambulance was cleaned, and response narratives needed to be written for departmental and medical documentation in the report room.

It wasn't long after we arrived. One of the Emergency Room doctors came into the report room and provided Ken and me with a patient update. Susan was doing great and responding well physically, and, with the arrival of her husband, hopefully starting her emotional healing. As for the twins, there was nothing the medical team could do. Nothing but simply standby once the twin's umbilical cords were severed. They were not viable and soon stopped moving after our arrival. They died.

As for our emotional healing, I can't speak for Ken, but I know I cried some large tears for a good amount of time. I'll never forget the emergency room doctor holding me in his arms in the report room. A therapist once told me firefighters, EMS, and police personnel have like a hazardous waste site within them. Emergency responses such as Susan's are sealed by responders in imaginary 55-gallon drums and placed in our personal waste dump site. Hopefully, it will be put away forever. Unfortunately, some of them will someday leak. Unfortunately, first responder personnel treat crying as a sign of emotional weakness. To seek outside assistance to work emotionally through these kinds of emergencies was frowned upon in those days. As for me, I can easily see why suicide and self-harm events among first responders are high.

Knowing your patients from a personal background is rare in the city environment. In small communities, it's far more common to know the very people firefighters and EMTs have been called to help. A shop owner, former schoolmate, coworker, and so on. How difficult it must be for them to recover from these events mentally.

It must be difficult to take these emotional traumas home to family members and struggle with needing support, but also a protective reluctance to share the disturbing details of the day. Easier to take the solitary path and try to put the day away inside, seeking instead a glass of whiskey or a cold bottle of beer for comfort, thereby numbing the emotional stresses.

In my later years at the United States Fire Administration, I realized the real heroes in the firefighter family are those men, women, and children welcoming them home and always standing ready behind their firefighters and EMTs to support their emotional well-being. Unfortunately, I didn't have the maturity or wisdom in my younger years to recognize enough of the importance of seeking emotional support from family and trained support counselors. I hope readers here will reach out for the emotional support you deserve in your times of need after life's bad call days. We all have them. Someone out there will listen and understand.

YOU ARE NEVER ALONE.

"The fire service is not about what you can do for yourself, it's about what you can do for others."

—Unknown

CHAPTER 11

RESPONSE TO GOTHAM CITY

It had been another busy day for our fire department. On Thursdays, for some reason, the fire department witnessed the number of emergency calls across the city ticking up over the past 5 years. This increase was particularly noticeable during the university's football season. As a result, there weren't many college classes on Fridays, and the university student body of about 45,000 enjoyed getting an early start on tailgating and tavern game-themed parties before weekend games.

It had been particularly busy for the department's medic units this Thursday. In addition to a home football game in the university's stadium, Fall had arrived, and mother nature had delivered a spectacularly colorful day. There were perfect temperatures, no humidity, and Fall colors on the trees across the city.

The calls for fire services and paramedic services varied this particular day. Car accidents during the morning commute and medical emergencies throughout the day. As with most busy days, getting a break to eat a meal was tricky. With every attempt by my partner Steve and me to eat something, the station Medic Unit was toned out. Our hot meal that day might have to be at a fast- food restaurant.

These dinner interruptions might also explain why firefighters and paramedics are terrible dinner guests. When one has been doing firefighter/EMS work, one tends to eat all your meals very quickly. Whether these first responders were on or off duty, meals were devoured before the next interruption.

So many lunches and dinners are interrupted by station tone-outs that first responders try to get in a hot fresh meal before sliding poles to the apparatus floor below. Some meals are just terrible when reheated in the microwave or kept warm in the oven—particularly dinners including fish. When attending off-duty meals with family and friends, firefighters will likely be waiting for dessert while everyone else at the table is still on their salads. This Thursday had been such a day. No sit-down meals.

Firefighters in our city eat two meals each day, always prepared by a firefighter on shift who enjoys cooking. The other firefighters on shift could be expected to fill a sous chef role to assist the cook. Our 24-hour shifts began at 7 am. After the equipment on the vehicles was checked, and Self-Contained Breathing Apparatus (SCBA) and other safety equipment were made ready, it was time for morning coffee with the firefighters of the day. This part of our day was typically where all the world's problems could be shared and solved. For example, our crew had solid expertise in relationship advice. Regardless of your marital or single status, there was no relationship issue, good or bad, that our crew couldn't solve for other firefighters.

During coffee, firefighters would piss and moan about the high cost of the meals the station cook was planning. It was a tradition to complain and throw anywhere from $5-$7 into that day's "food fund," depending on the menus for the two meals. Being the central downtown station with a staffing of eleven to thirteen on duty, the cooks usually had around $80 for two meals. That was enough in those days. Firefighters measure the national inflation by their daily food fund donations and nothing else.

What started when I was a rookie at $3 a day had become $6 and then $7, which meant food prices were rising. Not a good thing. After all of the crew bitching about money and food costs over cups of coffee, and while solving relationship problems, the day's cooks would go off to shop. Only to return to the station for the bitching to start again over the cooks' menus and food choices for the day. Some of the firefighters had no idea that the menus were not planned ahead. The menu selection of the day's meals was based entirely on the cost of meat.

In the middle of our station territory was a small family-owned grocery market that wasn't a part of any large chain store operation. Their unpackaged meat butcher services were of great value to our crew. Often the butchers would discount their meat prices for the firefighters. For example, the cost of seven pounds of hamburger might be reduced to the cost of two pounds. Likewise, a nine-pound rib roast might only be valued at two pounds, a significant chow fund savings. While one might expect a lawyer from City Hall to go crazy over these meat gift deals for firefighters, the firefighters saw it to be an intelligent business decision by the owner.

Everything else for the meals, like potatoes, noodles, and vegetables, cost full price. This practice ensured the store sales of about a hundred dollars every morning, 365 days a year. And as other stations became aware of the butcher's meat deals, it wasn't long before five or more additional station cooks were shopping at this small store each morning—big money for a small store for a little savings deal on meat.

One of the meat butchers, Jerry, asked my partner Steve and me during our food-shopping trip how he could become a paramedic. Unfortunately, only full-time commissioned (sworn in and badged) firefighters could become paramedics for the city then. Over the years, this has wonderfully changed, and it's common now to find countless noncommissioned men and women working in careers or volunteering on medic units across the nation.

At that time, when Jerry asked about becoming a certified paramedic, one was either an Emergency Medical Technician (EMT) or trained in Advanced Life Support (ALS) as a paramedic. Nowadays, EMTs have many other opportunities to acquire highly trained skills, such as IVs and intubation, and to be able to give some preapproved heavy-duty medications.

While we were considered career firefighters/paramedics for the city, our community was surrounded by some 20-25 volunteer fire and EMS departments. As paramedics were dual-trained as firefighters, Steve and I suggested that Jerry explore volunteer EMT opportunities with his local all-volunteer department where he lived. It was most admirable, and Steve and I were honored by our local meat butcher's desire to serve his community as a volunteer EMT during his hours away from the store. Jerry was a young man with a young family. He was trying to find ways to serve his community and experience new professional possibilities—an incredible young man with a life's dream.

As out-of-hospital care was gaining popularity, particularly with the popularity of the television show *Emergency*, the local Trade School College offered a robust EMT training curriculum for volunteers. It wasn't long before Jerry finished his 80 hours of EMT training and received his state and national certifications as an EMT. He immediately volunteered to serve on his local volunteer rescue squad.

Several months would pass before Jerry announced to the shopping firefighter cooks that he had achieved his state EMT instructor's certificate allowing him to train EMTs anywhere throughout the state. Within a couple of years, Jerry would no longer be a butcher. Instead, Jerry became a staff member of the state's Emergency Medical Services (EMS), thereby certifying EMTs, trainers of EMTs, and EMT curriculums starting at other state trade schools and including the state certification of paramedics. I know the career firefighters who shopped into his small store, watched Jerry chase his goals, and encouraged Jerry to feel significant pride in what Jerry had achieved.

Not long after finding himself in his new statewide EMS career, Jerry was recruited to join the state's Offices of Emergency Management (OEM). In just 10 years, Jerry had gone from his meat carving job to his new position responsible for all emergency management training and EMS training for the entire state. Jerry's journey is an all-inspiring story from a butcher to a volunteer EMT to service in one of the state's highest Emergency Management (EM) positions. He's retired now after a long and fulfilling career, but he's not too retired to help others reach their dreams. Jerry has spent a career paying it forward. Now Jerry teaches part-time for FEMA, the Federal Emergency Management Agency.

Lunch that day had been interrupted by a response to the University Union for a fight between two students leaving one with chipped teeth, a bloody nose, and what was sure to become a black and blue pair of raccoon eyes. Working closely with our police officers, we had the apparent loser soon patched up, loaded on a stretcher, and on their way to the local Emergency Room. I think the other ended up with silver bracelets.

Upon returning, dispatch requested a response to a local downtown intersection for a bicycle versus a car. This patient had a broken arm and scraps, lacerations, and bruises. Once treated, this patient was loaded into Medic 1 and on their way to another Emergency Room. After these calls and about 2 hours after the other firefighters sat for lunch without Steve and me, it could be concluded that reheated perch fillets and 3-hour-old French fries suck. These and other calls would fill out the rest of the day, including another tone right at dinner for a cardiac patient. Another meal 2 hours late.

Somewhere between 10-11 pm, the station tones sounded for an "unknown" emergency just a block and a half away from Station One. Steve and I had responded to many calls on Medic 1 that day. Who cared about the time? Even more frustrating was missing meals throughout the day and grabbing food from fast-food joints.

"Attention Medic 1, 402 Monroe Street for an unknown problem. Time out 10:39 pm."

Being a pregame Thursday night, law enforcement officers were busy running their many calls throughout the city and unavailable to respond with Medic 1. It was clear Steve and I would arrive on location well ahead of backup from law enforcement. As Medic 1 arrived on location on Monroe Street, the next-door neighbors were trying to explain to Steve and me the muffled yells and screams of a woman coming from the second floor of this residential home. My mind was racing with thoughts as we were walking into this kind of incident without police officers present. Our medical box offered little protection if someone had a gun or knife. I never liked walking into dark homes for medical calls without police.

The Deputy Fire Administrator (now retired) of the United States Fire Administration (USFA), Dr. Denis Onieal, was often heard reminding firefighters and students of the National Fire Academy (NFA), "Law enforcement deals with all threats presented by other people. When threatened by another person, law enforcement is called. Firefighters are first to respond when people are threatened by things (chemicals, burns, accidents, falls, cardiac, etc.)." Firefighters are not specifically trained to assist people and respond to emergencies exhibiting the presence of violence. However, we worked closely with officers when we needed to. When did you ever hear of someone being arrested by their local fire department? It happens, but it's extremely rare.

The front door of the house was locked, so Steve and I would have to use force to enter the home. While we were forcing the front doors, screams were confirmed coming from inside the residence. Forcing the front door wasn't a problem, except the owner was now stuck with front door repairs. When ladders company personnel force something open, they're typically not gentle.

When not on EMS calls, all paramedics in our department were also assigned to their station's ladder company in the event of fire responses. Paramedics in our department were duo-trained as both paramedics and firefighters. In summary, we were supplementing and rounding out the personnel needed for ladder work. Working with ladders companies, life safety/search and rescue, ventilation, and forced entry were among the responsibilities and skills trained to do by paramedics.

The muffled screaming of a struggling female was evident. It was coming from an upstairs bedroom. As Steve and I climbed the stairs to the second floor, we could see the bedroom door was closed. It wasn't locked. Entry was slow, not knowing what the hell was going on behind the door and without cops to assist us in the event the situation involved violence.

Upon entry to the bedroom, we discovered a completely nude young female, tied to all four corners of the bed, blindfolded with a towel or handkerchief lightly tied over her mouth. She was spread eagle on the bed, tied and crying for help. WTF? Did she tie herself up? Was she tied up and abandoned? Or, worst of all, had she been attacked and assaulted?

We announced immediately we were firefighters called by neighbors to help. As my partner and I removed her blindfold and the cloth covering her mouth and over her nose, she silently indicated there was something between the bed and wall under the window we needed to attend to. She began frantically pointing to the floor. Again, WTF? Was it the invader? Was it an angry husband or boyfriend? Gun? Knife?

Then the object of her desire for us to see was discovered. Between the bed and wall was a large gathering of black silk cloth with a black hood and hairy legs protruding from the strange pile of black on the floor. No violence. No guns. No knives. No fists. And indeed no movement by the individual on the floor. This was surprisingly, considering all the commotion in the room.

In a short time, the facts of our response became known. The female victim in the role of "damsel in distress" had been awaiting her rescue by her hero… Batman. All the while, she was tied to the bed frame. Our required skills and training for this situation, already on full display with the front door, would be adequate to handle this emergency.

First, Steve began untying the female while assuring her the evening's superhero would be okay. Then, as she went to get clothing, I focused on awakening the unconscious superhero. He was dressed head to toe in a realistic, complete Batman costume, and now the explanation became even more evident.

As the female awaited her superhero's arrival, Batman scaled their bedroom dresser and prepared to jump from the dresser top to the bed, thereby rescuing the poor female securely tied to the bed.

Unfortunately, when Batman made his heroic jump from the dresser top, he either hadn't planned on hitting the ceiling fan or the ceiling. No one knows what he hit, but he knocked himself "stone cold" out when he jumped. He had been out cold for 10-15 minutes before neighbors heard the young woman's attempts to get help and called 911. Oh, what firefighters can be asked to do to support our local superheroes?

Two ammonia inhalants quickly revived Batman and began clearing his head. Steve and I were surprised he had no ammonia inhalants in his Utility Belt. Fortunately, we did. We might have expected his first words to be "thank you," but no. Instead, Batman immediately asked if we were going to report this? "Will the media find out about this?" I also expected he might ask about the woman tied to the bed.

The young woman in distress reappeared clothed, and her first concern wasn't for poor Batman but for what the neighbors knew. Whom would we paramedics tell? Is this going to be a part of a public record somewhere? The young couple was assured that Steve and I wouldn't say anything other than a "citizen assist" on our report. We promised never to speak of their secret nor let anyone know the secret identity of Batman. Their secret was safe with us. They could keep their red faces, though.

We lied. Of course, the Station One firefighters would hear about the night we saved Batman. No longer that evening did we bitch about meals we missed, past patient cases, or wondering about the night's calls ahead. Instead, our banter on Medic 1 was focused on how many other firefighters and emergency room nurses on duty that night would hear about

Medic 1 saving Batman. How many individuals could we share our story and laugh with before the end of the shift?

Then there's the reality the entire city was without its superhero for a short period that night and how fortunate we were to save a damsel in distress. Did the couple we helped ever reflect on that night with laughter or blushes?

"Firefighters are the ones who are always willing to go above and beyond the call of duty."

—Anonymous

CHAPTER 12

MIDNIGHT SWIM IN LIVER POOL

I have never developed an affection for liver sausage. This German product has also been known by another name, Braunschweiger. I have only tried liver sausage once and choose never to be so grossed out again. It's a product made by mixing pork liver with enough ingredients to hide what other parts of the pig you're eating. So when mentioned, I turn the other way. Growing up, I thought it was my mother's punishment to have to eat Braunschweiger, or liver sausage.

Fire Station 8 is one of the oldest stations in our city. The station is tucked nicely into an old residential area. It has been the neighborhood's pride for almost 85 years—a place for neighboring residents to gather, meet and talk with station personnel. A place for kids to visit, have a soda pop on hot days, and climb on the fire apparatus. Firefighters are often seen sitting outside on chairs and benches in front of the station with the apparatus doors open and the fire trucks visible to residents of the neighborhood—a genuinely welcoming and old fire department cultural feel about Station 8.

Fire Station 8 was located strategically between a couple of main city thoroughfares providing quick access by Station 8 fire trucks to all parts of its first-run territory and the rest of the city. Getting to spend a day on duty at Station 8 was a reminder of the past station cultures of the fire department. One can only imagine the stories these Station 8 walls could tell.

Station 8 housed three fire response units. Engine 8, Ladder 8, and Medic 8 ran out of this station. Engine and Ladder 8 were among the oldest vehicles in the fire department's fleet. It was the practice in our department that newer, more powerful, and versatile vehicles were put first into service in the busier fire stations. As the fire trucks aged, usually around 15 years, they were replaced by newer state-of-the-art vehicles and then sent to the older, quieter stations. This procedure would allow the department's fleet maintenance program to gain another 5-10 years of service from these older fire trucks.

Medic 8 was much newer. As the department's paramedic program was only about 10 years old and carried Advanced Life Support (ALS) equipment, the medic units tended to be state-of-the-art vehicles and much newer.

There were three brass poles for firefighters to slide down to the apparatus floor from the station's upper floors. There was one in the kitchen, another in the second floor hallway, and a third in the middle of the bedroom, which all eight firefighters on duty 24/7 shared. The fire poles had a wooden cover.

One lifted the wooden cover on the floor to slide down the poles. A weighted pulley system in the ceiling ensured the cover opened quickly, exposing the apparatus floor below. One would then hug and tuck the pole into your shoulder, wrap a leg around the pole, and loosen one's arms to slide to the floor below. You came to a gentle stop on the floor next to the fire trucks by simply putting pressure on the pole with one's shoulder. And as always, you hoped you were fast enough not to have another firefighter come down on top of you.,

On a day when I had been detailed to Station 8, the officers had requested the crew to do some cleaning behind a group of old file cabinets. The cabinets were on the second floor, with about six cabinets lining a wall. All cabinets contained old records and the history of Station 8. One can only imagine what might be in those files, but not a good day to look. So the cabinets were pulled away from the wall for cleaning behind.

An old pay stub was found under one of the cabinets dated 1932. The total amount on the check was $172, a check dating from the Depression years. When we moved those files, firefighters in our department were paid every 2 weeks, so $172 wasn't bad for the depression years. However, what we thought was a bi-weekly paystub was a monthly check. Hard to believe individuals doing this kind of firefighter work for a little over $2,000 a year. Then again, time is what it was.

In station life, one firefighter will cook the crew's meals for the day, providing two meals, lunch around noon and dinner around 5 pm. The only variation from these two meals may be a large brunch on Sundays.

On this day, firefighter Megan was cooking for the station crew. For lunch, Megan made grilled cheese sandwiches and tomato soup with maggots (rice). Tomato soup and maggots were one of the cultural meals of the department of Campbell's tomato soup and small noodles (referred to by firefighters as maggots). Megan announced the evening meal would be stuffed pork chops, mashed potatoes, gravy, and green beans with a salad.

Stuffed pork chops "Megan style" involved preparing a large pan of hand-mixed stuffing, burying the browned pork chops in the mixed stuffing, and covering and baking for an hour. It was a great meal prepared by Megan. It added to an excellent time to continue discussing the 1932 paystub found earlier in the day.

Once meals were over and before dishes were washed, the crew typically would share a possible dessert and a cup of coffee. At this time, someone at the table noticed Megan's facial changes. Some on duty would say her face showed a sudden concern. Others on duty thought it was a sly smile. When asked, Megan explained she had a small cut on her finger from preparing lunch. She had treated it and covered her wound with a Band-Aid. She further explained the Band-Aid was no longer on her finger, and she must have lost it when she hand-mixed the stuffing.

Immediately, Station 8's hypochondriac, Roger, launched himself from his chair and headed to the pan containing the remainder of the evening meal. Frantically he grabbed a fork and spatula to begin digging through the pork stuffing. After a frantic 3–4-minute search Roger announced there was no Band-Aid, which could only mean one thing. Someone ate the band-aid. With such a great meal, some cared about the missing Band-Aid, and others didn't give it another thought. Too late to care, and Station 8 remained quiet that day. Until…

Attention Medic 8, 2300 Commercial Avenue, for an injured male. Time out, 0215."

We knew the address well; this was a large, 24/7 meat kill and packing operation and had long been a significant employer and community icon. Not to mention the wonderful neighborhood smells when they were smoking meats.

En route, we were advised by the 911 Communications Center to respond to the first aid station on the plant's site. There we would be met by company medical staff (at 2 am, usually, that would mean one nurse and security guard). Our 42-year-old patient was reported to be on the fourth floor of the processing building. Additionally, our patient was awake, alert, and oriented to person, place, and time.

Upon our arrival, we were met by a nurse who confirmed the patient was on the fourth floor. She added that the patient had fallen, and although she hadn't seen him yet, it sounded significant. The nurse further reported the individual had a back injury due to the fall. This information helped as my partner John and I could load up the cervical collars, backboard, and frac straps needed to immobilize the individual. Once loaded, we proceeded to the freight elevator for a trip to the fourth floor.

Once on the fourth floor, John and I were escorted down a long hallway into a large meat-processing room. Two large copper vats or containers were in this room, each 30-40 feet in diameter. Over and above the vats were catwalks for workers to access mixing equipment below and into the copper vats. Attached to the catwalks were two large slow-moving mixers, like people use to blend cake or cookie mixes. The only difference was these mixers were 9-10 feet tall and another 8 feet wide.

In each vat was a slurry of tan-covered liquid liver sausage. The smell was so disgusting. Standing in the middle of the first vat of liquid meat was a male worker standing with the meat slurry up to his chest. The vat was approximately 6 feet deep but filled with liquid meat to about 4 feet. When asked, the man, who could talk, indicated he couldn't move his legs and that his back was injured.

Given the patient's injured back and immobility problems, we couldn't lift him out of the vat and back onto the catwalk. He also indicated he couldn't move his legs enough to make it to the side of the vat. The only alternative was for John and me to enter the vat full of liquid meat and wade out to him. Unfortunately, we had been asleep 20 minutes ago and were now entering a vat of stinky, slimy liver sausage.

We entered the meat mixture from the side of the vat. Uniforms, shoes, badges, and clothes. The liver sausage was wet and quite warm. Not sure of the temperature of the meat, but it was at least 80 degrees. Possibly higher but comfortable for liver sausage. Before taking two steps, there was meat in our hair, our glasses, and anywhere you might think of, and it was all just gross. No other words but gross.

With the help of the company staff, we dropped a backboard from across the elevated catwalk to the patient's side. After two steps in the vat, carrying the backboard was a worthless idea. Actually, stupid idea comes to mind. Maybe, If we get on each side of our patient, we could walk him out of the meat. We walked with great effort through the meat to the patient's side. Our efforts worked. With assistance, he could walk to the side of the vat. With the help of staff, we could lift him out with us under him pushing and his fellow workers lifting from above. The patient lift had put John and my chins at the level of the liquid liver sausage meat.

I don't know if our entry into the vat and walking through the liver sausage slurry contaminated this batch of Braunschweiger or not. But, frankly, we didn't care. However, our uniforms, shoes, belts, and badges were full of liver sausage. The meat seemed to be in every pocket of our uniforms. And this was just the start of where this meat would spread.

It was most certainly on our equipment. Our stretcher. Our portable radio, for example. The only exception and, most importantly, this meat slurry had not found its way inside the medical box containing costly medications carried by city paramedics. Fortunately, this patient never required us to open the "drug box." We were relieved to see all the meat on the outside of the box. We breathed a loud sigh when we realized we hadn't contaminated the inside contents of the "drug box." That would have been costly damage.

As we left the mixing room and started toward the elevator, one couldn't help but notice the sloshing of meat in our shoes with each step. One also realized the meat was everywhere on our equipment and underwear. If there had been a cleanup facility on the fourth floor, it wasn't offered to us by the company staff.

Once loaded in the ambulance, the total contamination of the Medic 8 began. The trip to the hospital would take between 12-15 minutes at this time of the morning. Once the trip began, John covered the driver's compartment with liver sausage. The steering wheel, driver's seat and seatbelt, door handles, directional controls, warning light controls, and the medic unit's internal radio and siren controls were all covered in meat. It was everywhere—meat on everything.

Liquid Braunschweiger had made its way to the ambulance floor, cabinet covers, and rear bench in the patient compartment of Medic 8. It was so bad that the liver sausage dripped off the patient's clothing, the stretcher, and the backboard onto the Medic Unit 8 floor. Fortunately, the slurry never reached the EKG/Defibrillator equipment on board. This equipment was hospital-grade and very expensive. I was able to protect medic items inside the cabinets, but not so successful in protecting the outer cabinet surfaces, the rear radio equipment, and the ambulance bench seating.

As was the practice of all department paramedics, we radioed ahead to the hospital's ER to provide a patient report and the estimated arrival time. We also used radio communications to warn them ahead of time of the mess arriving along with our patient. We were concerned about what happened to our ambulance during the short ride to the emergency room. Therefore, inform emergency room staff about the Braunschweiger-covered patient and paramedics arriving at their front door.

When we arrived at the emergency room, we were met by the medical staff bearing gifts. Buckets of warm water, hospital gowns, and surgical foot coverings. All for cleaning liver sausage from our bodies. The emergency room staff were gowned head to foot in hospital hazardous material attire.

Once the patient was brought out of the ambulance, they were kind enough to wheel the patient into the hospital. We were to stay out until we had a chance to clean up.

Standing in the outdoor parking lot of the ER, John and I stripped down. Our clothing was placed into plastic garbage bags that the hospital maintenance staff provided for us. We washed what we could with the water provided and put on the hospital gowns to cover ourselves up. Once the chunks of meat and clothes were off, we were allowed into the emergency room. In hindsight, we should have called for the fire department's Haz-Mat decontamination equipment.

Once in the hospital, we were directed to the on-duty emergency room doctor's quarters, where we could shower and finish getting this crap off us. Staff provided us with new surgical scrubs for clothing to be able to return to Station 8, not the preferred clothing, but better than anything with stinky meat.

We decided not to return to service until we could deal with the mess inside the ambulance. Janitorial services provided some cleaning supplies to clean the driver's compartment. We also could clean the outside of the medical drug box and inspect it to ensure our cardiac monitoring equipment was okay for use. By now, it was 5:30 am, and we had had enough of the liver sausage.

We left the hospital after retrieving the stretcher and nothing else but our uniforms and shoes in trash bags. After a cup of coffee with the nursing staff and a few laughs over our early morning swim in liver sausage, we were on our way to fleet maintenance to retrieve a reserve ambulance. Reserve ambulances were secondary to older vehicles set up to be put in service at times like this when a front-line ambulance can no longer be used. With liver sausage still everywhere on this ambulance, there was no way we could have put another patient in it, much less ourselves.

After a 6-am exchange of medic units, we were back in service and returning to Station 8. Thank goodness the station remained quiet until the shift changed at 7 am. Given all we had were surgical attire and fire department boots for shoes, we might have scared any patients who may have called before 7 am. We had quite a story to tell the crew over morning coffee, and we were never so happy to be off duty finally. There's still some guilt about the liver sausage mess we left at Fleet Maintenance. We owe the department staff a great thanks and apologies for the mess John and I left them with. Sorry.

"The best way to find yourself is to lose yourself in the service of others."

—Mahatma Gandhi

CHAPTER 13

MY OWN FINE RED LINE SAINT FLORIAN, "PLEASE HELP ME !"

Living with two other firefighters after only 2 months on the job, I had grown accustomed to hearing about their fires, high volumes of emergency response, and their tough calls. When we came out of basic firefighter training, while my roommate Steve and Rick were assigned busy stations downtown, I was sent to what was affectionately known as the "retirement home" of the department—no calls and nothing but "old-timers" riding out their careers.

I could speak of the false alarms and the countless car accidents I'd been to as a probationary firefighter. Still, the only fire I'd seen so far was in a garbage truck. The contents had caught fire and, to extinguish them, they were emptied on the street. So we spent an hour and a half walking around in garbage, putting out small fires. Hardly an eyebrow was raised whenever I mentioned my garbage conflagration to my roommates, who had already been fighting active residential interior fires and responding to calls at all hours during their shifts.

Finally, on a cold Saturday night, it happened. My first fire call had finally arrived. My first potential fire.

"Attention Station 5 Complete, Engine 8. Engine 3 and Car 31, 1603 Camden Road for the report of a basement fire. Occupants are evacuating. Time out 10:33 pm."

Thankfully, Ralph was riding on the Engine 5 tailboard with me that day. While suiting up in my firefighting gear, Ralph, a veteran firefighter, could sense my excitement and constantly reminded me about my next steps. Pull up your boots. Put on your gloves. Tighten your helmet strap. Be sure to buckle your tailboard safety belt. We were moving fast to get on the fire truck, and Ralph was most respectfully and thankfully understanding my excitement,

There was a time in the past when firefighters rode hanging onto a bar on the rear tailboard of the fire vehicle. It exposed them to all elements but was an exciting place to be. Once onboard the vehicle, the firefighters would wrap a canvas strap around their waists and secure themselves to the fire engine with a large carabiner. Then, you pushed a button that sounded in the cab and indicated to the officer and driver that the rear firefighters were ready to go.

Once we pulled out of the station behind Ladder 5 and ahead of Medic 5, Ralph was so helpful. On this day, my first task at the fire would be to "make the hydrant." In other words, attach a hose line to a fire hydrant to ensure an adequate and secure water supply to Engine 5. Throughout the 2-3-mile trip to the residential fire, Ralph reviewed several times repeatedly the steps necessary to complete my hydrant responsibilities.

Pulling off the main thoroughfare that 5 Complete (Ladder 5, Engine 5, and Medic Unit 5) had used to get to the fire building quickly; you could smell the odor of a burning structure in the air. Once Engine 5 pulled onto the street, we could see the smoke visible throughout the neighborhood from the tailboard. Once Engine 5 was parked in front of the building, we could see the smoke pouring out of the basement window wells and several first-floor windows. I was never so thankful for the time Ralph took with me. I felt anxious and nervous, and thanks to Ralph, I was at the same time ready for my officer's assignments as Ralph reviewed my initial steps.

The building we were called to was a four-unit apartment building. The building was on the corner of a long line of 4-unit apartments. Being on the corner meant the hydrant for the water supply was within 15 feet of Engine 5. As Engine 5 came to a halt, 20 feet behind Truck 5. Lieutenant Walter stood up in the cab and instructed the driver to make the hydrant and Ralph and me to advance a preconnect hose line into the building. When filled with water, a preconnect hose line was an inch and a half in diameter. This hose was already connected to Engine 5 and could be rapidly advanced into the building and to the seat of the fire.

Ralph and I knelt down with our hose at the front door of the four-unit. Ralph began putting on his mask and turning on his SCBA air supply. He reminded me to do the same, and Ralph gave me a once-over to be sure I was properly ready to go. Once the air was turned on, a firefighter was supposed to have a 30-minute air supply. Heavy breathing and exertion would make 20 minutes more realistic; with a limited air supply, you also needed to leave yourself enough air to get out of the building as well as enter the building.

Ralph and I crawled down the smoke-filled hallway feeling for a door that would lead us to the basement and fire below. We could hear other firefighters working elsewhere in the building. They were looking for fire victims and openings to help ventilate the building by getting the smoke-filled air out and allowing fresh air to enter the building.

There were only three doors on the first floor and a stairwell—two for apartments and the third leading to the basement. The stairwell led to the second floor. We found that basement door quickly. It was unlocked, allowing Ralph and I to quickly descend into the basement's heat, smoke, and dreadful black darkness from the wooden stairs. Basement fires are no different from fighting a fire in a bank vault. And it was hot from the yet undiscovered fire.

Although we couldn't see an inch in front of us, we had stepped into a maze of some kind. There were large boxes everywhere we turned. The boxes everywhere were confusing and added to the difficulty of finding the fire. We would learn later one of the new residents of the building had recently downsized from a residential home into a small apartment. He needed additional storage space for more stuff than his apartment could hold. He was using the basement as temporary storage until a more permanent solution could be found.

Real fire in a building is nothing like fires seen on television or in movies. In a building with depleted oxygen levels, the fire appears more like one you would see at the bottom of a barbeque pit. Nothing but a red glow until oxygen is introduced into the environment. Although a simplified description, real fire in an unventilated structure is not something you walk up to and put water on. Firefighters have to find the fire. As firefighters working above us on the upper floors began ventilating the building, more and more fire would be found and extinguished with improved oxygen levels.

Crawling on our hands and knees, Ralph and I had just reached what we believed was the base of the fire when a large bang was heard. The sounds of the crashing and splintering of wood followed the loud sound. It wasn't an explosion but a noise loud enough to get our attention. Suddenly the fire seemed to surround us completely. Not only had a resident stored personal belongings but also flammable liquids in the basement. The flammable liquid had been stored under the very stairs we had entered from. This fire had finally reached this new fuel supply, and with the collapse of the stairs and partial collapse of the first floor, Ralph and I were trapped.

At this point, Ralph yelled for us to get out of the basement. With that, we began to crawl on our hands and knees, following the hose line we had dragged into the basement. Firefighters know when they're in trouble to follow the hose line, which ultimately leads back to the engine it's attached to.

Until now, we hadn't known the first floor had partially collapsed, and the basement stairs had burned through. And to make matters worse, Ralph and I were running out of air. Our masks were vibrating, a sign of low air for firefighters. The vibration of the mask was a safety feature of the SCBA to let you know when your air is running low. Holy shit,

I'm about to die in my first fire!! So scared, I yelled, "Saint Florian, don't let me die!"

Why is Saint Florian the Patron Saint of firefighters? Legend says during his life, St. Florian put out a massive fire with only one bucket of water, saving a village from ruin. St. Florian is depicted in artwork pouring water from a bucket or small vessel. Many years after St. Florian's death, a man said he was saved from a deadly fire when he called on St. Florian, begging for his intercession.

With this next paragraph, you can accept it as the fact it is or say bullshit.

Just then, as we were trying to figure out a way out of this basement fire, I saw, walking through the smoke, a faint figure in human form. It was just the outline of a figure simply walking toward us. The figure's hands were open, and I only remember a calm coming over me and what seemed a sudden clarity of thought. Thoughts of frantic escape from dying became calming thoughts for Ralph and me. We were going to be okay. I know what I saw in that basement that October night. But, until now, I've never shared this with my family or with the thousands of firefighters I've had the honor to meet in my 50-year career in the fire service.

Just then, as this figure appeared in the smoke, the sound of an aluminum ladder was heard directly in front of Ralph. It almost hit him on the head. And just like that, we heard Engine 3 firefighter Dale's voice calling for us to come to the ladder. Engine 3 had arrived, and the leadership on the outside realized Ralph and I were in trouble when the first floor partially collapsed. So Engine 3's firefighters dropped a small aluminum ladder into the basement where the stairs had been. Dale was a well-known member of Station 3 and a most welcomed voice. Ralph and I were up the ladder and safe in seconds.

As with all fire departments, there's still much to do once the fire is extinguished. For example, searching for any chance of further fires. Being called back to a fire for a rekindle is a source of fire service embarrassment. Once a fire is out, another fire shouldn't reignite.

There was significant overhaul and salvage at this fire. Firefighters were looking behind ceilings and walls for possible fire extensions, replacing and cleaning equipment used in firefighting activities, helping residents possibly locate pets, and possibly retrieving valuable documents. The list of possible tasks following a fire is lengthy. Firefighting doesn't end because there's no more flame or smoke.

It was a very quiet ride on the back of Engine 5 following the fire. I don't know if this was due to what Ralph and I had gone through or if I had done anything wrong. We had rolls of used hose stacked on the tailboard, and this hose would have to be unloaded when we got back to the station.

Once back to Station 5, the hose was unloaded for cleaning by the next day's oncoming crew. New air tanks were placed in service on our SCBAs and checked for future use—a list of tasks needed to be completed before retiring to our bunks for whatever sleep remained. But as always, it was a traditional time for a cup of coffee in the kitchen with the Station 5 crew to celebrate a successful firefight and share observations.

While drinking coffee and talking about my first fire as a rookie, there came the point when Ralph leaned over to me and asked a question that has stayed with me since 1974. Ralph's exact words were, "Tom, did you....?" He hadn't even finished the question before I responded, "YES!"

I had thought I was crazy and afraid to even mention it for fearing the ridicule of my fellow crew members. But Ralph had seen the same figure as I did. To this day, I cannot explain what I saw, nor can Ralph. But we both saw the figure in the smoke while crawling in the burning basement that October night.

How does one go home and tell your family you came within minutes or seconds of dying in a fire? So I think I filed this one under "Yeah we had a fire last night, and we put it out."

It may have been intended to be a lesson. At age 21, I had stepped up to my own fine red line. The same fine red line between life and death that I would spend my life protecting others from crossing. The very fine red line the men and women of the volunteer and career fire service dedicate themselves to protecting. Getting to the fine line between life and death was easy, and I was taught the value of needing to rely on others to be safe. I would spend the rest of my life looking to the left of me and to the right of me, willing to protect those same individuals looking over me. I love to imagine a world where everyone looks to the left and right of them and takes care of those they see.

Volunteer and Career firefighters are not superheroes. They are, instead, extraordinary individuals dedicated to the care of those around them, knowing they can also depend on those men and women around them to do the same for them.

CONCLUSION

MESSAGE FROM THE AUTHOR

Thank you for allowing me to share a few stories from my fire service portfolio. Across this nation, over 1.1 million men and women serve the safety needs of all of America. Over 70% of these special individuals are volunteers in their local Fire and EMS services, each of them with a portfolio of stories from experience. Some have stories far more tragic than the ones I've shared, and yes, some are even more unique and humorous.

There's no location in the U.S. without protection from a fire and an EMS department. And if you should ever call 911, you can be assured these trained men and women will respond regardless of the scope and scale of your emergency. Whether the emergency is on a catastrophic scale, such as tornados, floods, acts of terrorism, Mass Casualty Incidents; or smaller scale, such as broken bones, medical, or simply a child locked in a bathroom, your fire department responds. So it's safe to say the men and women of both volunteer and career departments will be there when called on your worst day ever. They are dedicated to your protection, recovery, and safety.

What makes these men and women so extraordinary is their commitment and dedication to ensuring the safety and well-being of all others. Most emergency callers are unknown before these firefighters and EMS personnel arrive on the scene. Know this about your firefighters.

You can ***TRUST*** firefighters to arrive as quickly as possible. You can be further assured they will arrive with unmeasured ***COMPASSION*** for all involved in the emergency. You can depend on these special men and women to arrive at solutions and action to provide the ***STABILITY*** required for you to survive and recover from your emergency. And finally, know that the ***HOPE*** for a safer community can be found in these men and women serving in all volunteer and career fire and EMS departments. After reading these chapters about fire service from my life, I hope you will feel a deeper appreciation for all they do for us. Thank you for sharing my stories.

Please support the firefighters looking out for your safety and that of your loved ones. They need your support as much as you need theirs.

ABOUT THE AUTHOR

Tom Olshanski has been a member of the fire service for 50 years in multiple roles. He has served in both volunteer and career firefighter departments. His last 20 years have been spent as the Director of External Affairs for the United States Fire Administration. Tom has received two-lifetime achievement awards. One was from the Nation Association of Government Communicators, and the second was from the Florida Fire Chiefs Association, Public Information Group. Tom has been an adjunct instructor for numerous courses for FEMA's Emergency Management Institute (EMI) since 1989. He has authored many courses and participated in many efforts to prepare community safety personnel for events such as the World Cup Soccer (1994), Super Bowls, Olympics, and National Political Conferences. Tom has also been involved in some large-scale national emergencies, Hurricanes Floyd, Katrina, and Sandy, including numerous other flooding and tornado storms. And September 11th. This short and brief listing makes it easy to see why he has been an often-called-upon conference speaker, seminar presenter, high-level speech writer, and frequent media guest. In 2004, Tom presented the mantra "*Everyone Goes Home*" to the

National Fallen Firefighter Foundation. Tom has committed throughout his career to "*Get the RIGHT information, to the RIGHT people, at the RIGHT time so that individuals can make the RIGHT decision to protect and ensure their safety and the safety of loved ones*".

You can contact Tom Olshanski at: usfachief@gmail.com.

www.ingramcontent.com/pod-product-compliance
Lightning Source LLC
LaVergne TN
LVHW090609110826
845146LV00001B/319

* 9 7 9 8 8 9 1 0 9 0 5 4 5 *